STUFF THEY DON'T WANT YOU TO KNOW

STUFF THEY DON'T WANT YOU TO KNOW

BEN BOWLIN

with Matthew Frederick and Noel Brown
HOSTS OF THE HIT PODCAST

STUFF
YOU
SHOULD
READ
An iHeart
Book

FLATIRON
BOOKS
NEW YORK

www.flatironbooks.com

The Library of Congress Cataloging-in-Publication Data
is available upon request.

ISBN 978-1-250-26856-3 (paper over board)
ISBN 978-1-250-26857-0 (ebook)

Our books may be purchased in bulk for promotional, educational, or
business use. Please contact your local bookseller or the Macmillan
Corporate and Premium Sales Department at 1-800-221-7945,
extension 5442, or by email at MacmillanSpecialMarkets@macmillan.com.

First Edition: 2022

10 9 8 7 6 5 4 3 2 1

Conspiracy Theory

The belief in an orchestrated strategy, involving three
or more parties working in secret toward some defined
goal—usually nefarious, always evident through the
correct recognition of certain events connected via a
larger, obsessively curated narrative.

Conspiracy Realism

The observation that some, but not all, conspiracy theories
have a partial basis in proven events—the realization
that, through the use of critical thinking, it is possible
to differentiate between fiction and fact.

CONTENTS

G **ATHER ROUND.** Let's trade spooky stories. Here's one you may have heard:

Your government is lying to you.

It's true. It's happening right now. As you encounter these words, some part of your livelihood is supporting a war started by powerful people you'll never meet, somewhere you will never go, extracting some resource you will never use, calling dibs on some land you will never see.

"What can we do?"

It's an age-old question in an age-old conflict: the people versus the powerful. The faceless many versus the shadowy few. No matter a government's size or structure, power inevitably becomes concentrated in the hands of a few decision-makers. Throughout history this fact has given rise to stories—some true, many false—of secretive, unaccountable factions that manipulate the levers of power to their own advantage.

As the world has grown smaller and more connected, the imagined reach of these shadowy cabals has grown. Today they guide global politics and media. They steer the economy both domestically and abroad. Their minions, groomed in exclusive, elite institutions all over the world, ply their trade in cloakrooms and country clubs and hunting lodges and private jets at 51,000 feet. They assume any number of names and labels— the Zoroastrians, the Knickerbockers, the Kabbalists, the Bilderbergs, the Globalists, the Illuminati, or, simply, Old Money. And it doesn't stop there. According to countless stories shared on social media platforms, these elites also worship Satan. They traffic in children. They even cannibalize their victims, so that they can harvest adrenochrome from their blood, a chemical purported to have life-extending properties. Why? So that they might live forever—presumably as our immortal overlords.

In 2015, one story goes, rogue patriots within the American military leadership recruited a New York businessman named Donald Trump for his second shot at the presidency. Trump was the only guy who could drain the swamp that is the US government of its corruption. He would root out, unmask, and punish these sinister elites, purifying the political world in advance of a reckoning called "The Storm." After Trump's surprising election in 2016, the sinister elites fought back. Pulling the puppet strings of society from their privileged positions within journalism, academia, Big Tech, and "the Deep State," they formed a conspiracy of their own, with the goal of stealing the 2020 election from President Trump. So desperate were they to eliminate the single greatest threat to their safety, anonymity, and quest for control, they took extraordinary measures. Their Trojan horse: the COVID-19 pandemic.

This is the core claim of the QAnon conspiracy theory.

If it doesn't ring a bell, congratulations. You have avoided the worst corners of the internet, talk radio, and cable news since 2017, when the initial details of the most recent "elite plan" for world domination came to light. This conspiracy theory took wing on internet forums like 4chan, where an anonymous poster (or posters) writing under the moniker "Q" looked out on the informational landscape and saw something that defied a commonsense explanation. All these mainstream, primarily liberal, factions of society were angrily and universally arrayed in opposition to Donald Trump's administration. It was, Q thought, too coordinated. Something else had to be going on. Something nefarious.

When we consider the bigger picture, it's no surprise a conspiracy theory like this would arise in the United States. The country itself is, after all, a child of conspiracy—a nation founded thanks to a successful conspiracy against British rule. Today residents of the US call those original lawmakers the "Founding Fathers," but the European monarchies of their day called them conspirators and traitors.

All of which is to say that the United States is no stranger to the language of conspiracy. And it has become increasingly fluent over the last one hundred years as its government has shown itself, again and again, to be worthy of skepticism and mistrust. This is what has made QAnon and countless other conspiracy theories, a number of which we will cover in this book, so believable to so many.[1] Their central claims of government malfeasance can often be traced back to some sort of true historical antecedent.

The highest levels of American government *have* been filled with people from elite institutions who were sometimes also members of secret societies.[2] Government agencies *have* performed unethical experiments on people without their consent and surreptitiously exposed people to biowarfare tests. Uncle Sam *has* waged war under false pretenses. The Central Intelligence Agency *has* conducted covert surveillance campaigns. Multiple administrations *have* hidden information—about UFOs, advanced weapons systems, imminent threats, and conflicting financial interests that may impact policy decisions. The governments of the world *do* operate clandestine programs from secret locations. They *have* spread propaganda at home and abroad. Government officials across the planet *have* engaged in unethical lobbying practices and backroom horse-trading in pursuit of personal agendas that didn't necessarily align with the interests of their constituencies. The United States of America *has overthrown* sovereign governments. They *have* inserted themselves into the global narcotics trade to launder the money and traffic the weapons needed to achieve those aims.

These disturbing facts provide fertile soil for increasingly bizarre speculation, complicated by the current confusion surrounding the term "conspiracy theory." In casual conversation, people often use the word

---

[1]   In a 2020 NPR/Ipsos poll, 17% of respondents believed the core QAnon theory was true and 37% weren't sure. Fewer than half of the respondents said it was false.

[2]   The US Supreme Court has had 115 justices in its 232-year history. Thirty-nine of those justices—more than one-third of the Court's total membership—attended one of three Ivy League law schools: Harvard, Yale, or Columbia. Currently, eight of the nine sitting justices attended either Harvard or Yale Law School.

"theory" as a way of articulating a hunch based on previous experiences or beliefs. This falls far short of the more rigorous, scientific definition of a theory. In the world of science, a theory is a carefully reasoned explanation for observations in the natural world, and this explanation is constructed using the scientific method, bringing to bear multiple facts and hypotheses. Scientific theories play a fundamental role in how we regard and understand the world around us. Evolution, relativity, and heliocentricity are all examples of scientific theory and nowhere as easy to dismiss as, say, the conspiracy theory that half-human reptilian aliens rule human civilization. While the vast majority of the world's population agrees scientific theories are largely sound, people often dismiss a conspiracy theory out of hand, simply because of the term applied to what it describes.

> In the world of science, a theory is a carefully reasoned explanation for observations in the natural world, and this explanation is constructed using the scientific method, bringing to bear multiple facts and hypotheses.

But why? What is it about these two words that wields such power over a person's opinion? The unfortunate truth is simply this: the modern definition of a "conspiracy theory" has transformed over time—now it is often (mistakenly) assumed to be a synonym for something both wildly untrue and easily dismissed. All musicians are members of some sort of Illuminati, for example, or Elvis Presley, Tupac Shakur, and Adolf Hitler all faked their deaths. Bigfoot is real, and, for some reason, very powerful people want to make sure this remains a secret.

Each of those examples alludes to claims that are, for the most part, easily debunked. Yet there are genuine, provable conspiracies—many of which, in their day, were also dismissed as conspiracy theories. The power of the phrase itself functions as a thought-terminating cliché. For many folks watching the news, reading social media, or speaking with their loved ones, hearing something described as a conspiracy theory automatically detracts from the credibility of the claims. This is both convenient and dangerous. Of course the world would be a simpler, possibly happier place if just calling something untrue made it so. But that is not the world we live in.

This book explores genuine conspiracies and the conspiracy theories that spring from them. It separates fact from fiction while, most importantly, arming the reader with the tools and techniques necessary to differentiate between the two out in the real world.

Why do so many government-related conspiracy theories seem plausible? Because the US government has actively, provably lied about its actions in the past. If it actually did *that*, the argument goes, why couldn't it do *this*? The simplicity of this logic is intoxicating, because the undeniable reality of our world is that governments lie. They obfuscate. They prevaricate. It doesn't matter who you are or where you live, the collection of bureaucrats, administrators, and political leaders who make up your country's government have deceived you in the past and are almost certainly deceiving you in some way right now—whether by omission or by commission. We can't begin to understand the phenomenon of conspiratorial thinking without first understanding the real stories of government deception that have made them possible.

This leads to the first of the three big questions this book will explore: Why? Why is your government lying to you and why do they lie about the things they lie about? In the pages that follow, we endeavor to answer that question by exploring the relationship and the differences between historical conspiracies and current conspiracy theories in nine different areas: biowarfare, human experimentation, surveillance, UFOs, propaganda, coups and assassinations, secret societies, political corruption, and drugs.

The second big question we address is baked into that exploration: How and why do conspiracy theories emerge? What are the conditions that make a conspiracy theory especially appealing to people? Like a hurricane or a tornado, conditions must be perfect to get things spinning in the right (or in this case, wrong) direction.

In charting the why and the how of conspiracy theories in these nine areas, we then turn to the third big question: How can the average person more reliably discern fact from fiction when confronted with a conspiracy theory? It's not enough to know why governments lie or how conspiracy theories develop; you need to know how to protect yourself from falling victim to either of them.

As you'll see, this book is not reflexively dismissive of conspiracy theorists. Dismissing a claim offhand shows a lack of both curiosity and critical thinking. (It's also a poor way of convincing a misguided person that their beliefs are in error.) Instead, we take these theories seriously, exploring their claims and acknowledging the facts upon which they are premised. Once the kernel of truth that exists at the heart of most conspiracy theories is understood, we can then challenge the typically grand assumptions, connections, and conclusions that inevitably follow. If the ideas spread by a given theory seem poisonous, we can use our understanding of critical thought to help keep our loved ones—and ourselves—from falling into the proverbial rabbit hole.

Unfortunately, too few journalists in today's society want to seriously interrogate conspiracy theories. It is easy to mock the misled or to ridicule people whose deep distrust of those in power has made them susceptible to outlandish beliefs. We often don't take the time to untangle the web of claims comprising a conspiracy theory like QAnon. We don't want to make the effort to trace the theory back to its roots or to understand how it materialized in popular culture. We are reluctant to look at the world through the eyes of a QAnon follower and see what they see. It is much simpler to other-ize them and paint them all with the same unflattering brush that Jake Angeli, aka the QAnon Shaman, used to paint his face when he and thousands of like-minded people breached the United States Capitol on January 6, 2021.

We do this at our peril.

In this book, we are going to buck that trend. We are going to take the historical conspiracies and the current conspiracy theories discussed in each chapter at face value, then we are going to dissect them, disassembling each claim until we're able to discern conspiracy fact from conspiracy fiction. When you finish reading this book, you will be able to identify the true stuff. The stuff they don't want you to know.

Let's begin. As we say in our podcast: here's where it gets crazy.

CHAPTER ONE

BIOLOGICAL WARFARE

YOU'RE STANDING OUTSIDE. THE SUN IS BRIGHT. THE SKY IS CLEAR. THE AIR IS WARM. THE WIND IS CALM. Out of your peripheral vision you spot an airplane. It soars past silently, 35,000 feet up, traveling at more than 500 miles per hour. There's no way to tell where it's coming from or where it's going. All you know for certain is that there are two, maybe four, long streamers of tightly formed clouds that extend back several miles from the trailing edge of the plane's wings. The clouds seem to just be hanging there, suspended, increasing in length as the plane moves farther away and eventually out of sight. Then you realize the long lines of clouds are also very slowly increasing in height and spreading in width, merging ultimately into one large gauzy blanket of cloud cover.

These are condensation trails, or contrails. They are clouds of ice crystals that form instantaneously when hot gases emitted in the exhaust from a plane's engines meet water vapor present in the supercold air of the upper atmosphere. Contrails can dissipate within a matter of moments or they can remain in the air for hours, depending on the combination of temperature and humidity at whatever altitude a plane is flying.

Contrails were discovered in the 1920s during some of the earliest high-altitude flights at the dawn of jet engine technology. They've been captured in photos as far back as 1940, and much of the science that explains them has been settled for decades. A paper produced for the American Meteorological Society in 1953 by a scientist named H. Appleman laid out the exact environmental conditions required for the development of contrails[1] and included a framework for understanding the circumstances under which a contrail would linger for an extended period of time. "Persist" is the word they use. If the air is damp and the temperature is minus 40 degrees Fahrenheit or colder—conditions that typically exist beginning above 25,000 feet—contrails are likely to persist for upward of thirty minutes to an hour on their own, and potentially several hours longer, if wind speed, wind direction, air pressure, and solar heating play along. Needless to say, it is a tightly bounded set of criteria and a narrow band of atmospheric conditions within which persistent contrails can exist.

Or so the government would have you believe.

As much as 40 percent of the US population would beg to differ.[2] According to the doubters, there is a major difference between the clouds that dissipate quickly and the ones that don't seem to go anywhere. The latter aren't contrails at all, they will tell you; they are *chem*trails. And they aren't full of ice crystals made of water vapor and engine exhaust detritus;

---

[1] The graph that pilots and meteorologists still use to predict contrails is called the Appleman Chart.

[2] In 2010, 2.6% of Americans believed that chemtrails were "completely" real and 14% partly believed they were real. By the fall of 2016, those figures had grown to 10% and 20–30%, respectively.

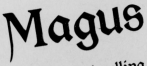

Magus

Buying and selling used books in Seattle since 1978

MagusBooksSeattle.com
magus@seanet.com

he government is dispersing for a number of
. You can tell the difference between chem-
t just by their quality but by their quantity.
ir thickness and their staying power. They
nd in recent years, proponents argue, mul-
in the same patches of sky, like they never
ections and creating a latticework or grid-
nts—clearly to maximize coverage. The
raphic concentration of trails is a more
ccording to some, that these persistent
ccurring environmental phenomenon.
and government controlled. They are

1990s after the United States Air
Force odification titled "Weather as a Force
Multi 025." Produced as a kind of thought
exercis well Air Force Base in Montgomery,
Alabam g in the paper's executive summary:

The line a strategy for the use of a
future o achieve military objectives …
A high weather modification offers a
dilemm unlike the splitting of the atom. While some segments
of society will always be reluctant to examine controversial issues
such as weather modification, the tremendous military capabilities
that could result from this field are ignored at our own peril.

This report was released to the public on August 1, 1996. Just five days
earlier a bomb exploded at Centennial Park during the Summer Olympics
in Atlanta. The month prior to that the Khobar Towers in Saudi Arabia
were bombed, killing nineteen US military personnel. All summer the US
had been lobbying the international community to support missile strikes
against Iraq because they wouldn't disarm. In March 1996, the Chinese

military was scaring everyone by playing war games with their missiles off the coast of Taiwan.

High risk, high reward? A dilemma not unlike splitting the atom? Tremendous military capabilities? Ignored at our own peril?

A RESOLUTION TO SHOW RESOLVE

It's widely understood today that the Gulf of Tonkin Resolution pushed through Congress by President Lyndon Johnson in August 1964 was largely a political maneuver designed to shore up Johnson's anticommunist credentials against Barry Goldwater, his notoriously bellicose Republican opponent in that year's presidential race.

Passed on August 7 and enacted into law three days later, the resolution was a response to a pair of "deliberate, unprovoked attacks" on two US destroyers less than a week earlier by North Vietnamese gunships in the Gulf of Tonkin. The resolution allowed Johnson to circumvent Congress in the deployment of conventional military forces in Southeast Asia, effectively giving the President unilateral war powers.

There was only one problem: as you will learn in Chapter 5, the second attack—the one LBJ relied upon to convince Congress to draft and pass the resolution—never happened. What did happen, barely two weeks earlier, was the nomination of Barry Goldwater as the Republican Party candidate for president in the upcoming election. What would happen three weeks later, was Johnson's nomination as the Democratic Party candidate.

Of the two, Johnson was the far superior operator in the realm of domestic policy. On foreign policy, however, Goldwater was a rabid right-wing anti-communist who couldn't have been more hawkish about nuclear weapons if he had a beak for a nose and talons for toes. Johnson believed that if he could show the electorate he was at least as tough as Goldwater on America's communist enemies, he could sufficiently diminish Goldwater's advantage in that area and win in a landslide. He was right. LBJ won 61% of the popular vote and 486 electoral college votes—the biggest rout since 1820.

Doesn't that sound like the government knows something we don't? It wouldn't be the first time a sitting president put the country on a war footing to firm up their chances of reelection. To a strong skeptic of the government, that description and those circumstances raise more red flags than an International Workers' Day march. They certainly did for a journalist from the Environment News Service named William Thomas. Thomas, a noted fringe science enthusiast, seized on the report as part of a story he published in January 1999, speculating about the cause of a rash of mysterious health problems afflicting people who had been exposed to what he termed "elaborate cross-hatched patterns . . . [of c]ontrails spread by fleets of jet aircraft." For the article, Thomas spoke to a number of the afflicted. They complained of watery eyes and runny noses, coughing spells, joint stiffness, shortness of breath, lingering respiratory infections, and even lupus. It could not be a coincidence, they believed to a person, that just prior to their falling ill, contrails created by jets had appeared in the skies. In all their years, they'd never seen contrails like these before.[3] That had to mean something.

Thomas then identified a number of the goals and predictions outlined in the air force report that could begin to explain these unusual contrail patterns. Among them were the pursuit of storm creation and storm modification, as well as the belief that "airborne cloud generation and seeding" could be effective in intensifying storm systems as a way to alter or control a battlespace. Some of these technologies were already being developed, Thomas reported. If that wasn't disconcerting enough, he also talked to a former engineer at the defense contractor Raytheon about the purpose of a joint military radio transmitter aimed at the ionosphere that had been under construction in Alaska since 1993. Named as only a government project can be, the Ionospheric Research Instrument (IRI) was part of the High Altitude Auroral Research Program (HAARP) and was designed to

---

[3] This is a key feature of the argument for the existence of chemtrails. Chemtrail conspiracists say that in the past contrails dissipated much more quickly. What, they ask, explains this change?

send a high-frequency radio signal into the ionosphere to see how it might disrupt the natural processes that occur that high up and to potentially "steer sections of the upper atmosphere." What made these two nascent atmosphere-related projects even more intriguing to Thomas, one could infer from his writing, is that they followed on the heels of a patent application submitted in 1990 by another defense contractor, Hughes Aircraft Company, for a method called "Stratospheric Welsbach Seeding" that aimed to shoot reflective particles into the cloud layer of the upper atmosphere in order to bounce some of the sun's ultraviolet rays back out to space, thereby reducing global warming caused by the greenhouse effect.[4]

What Thomas has here, then, are three government-connected entities with military, environmental, and one could argue, *existential* objectives, talking about messing around with bleeding-edge technologies in every important layer of the atmosphere in an effort to understand, alter, or control it—all within a few years of each other. For a skeptic and a journalist like Thomas, who is also incentivized in this moment to find an explanation that validates the suspicions of the sick people who have trusted him with their story, this trio of technological advancements is a pattern too rich to ignore. What's that line from Ian Fleming? "Once is happenstance. Twice is coincidence. Three times is enemy action."[5] In 1999, the assumptions held by Thomas and the people he interviewed weren't quite so dark or adversarial as they have become.[6] Public trust in the government was much higher in the late '90s than it is today. But the fact that the government would publish

> **Once is happenstance. Twice is coincidence. Three times is enemy action.**
>
> **—IAN FLEMING**

---

[4] In a fitting twist, this patent was assigned to Raytheon in 2004, before expiring in 2010.

[5] Fleming is the creator of James Bond.

[6] Roughly bookended by two Gulf Wars instigated by presidents named Bush, the 1990s are generally regarded as a very peaceful decade.

a report like "Weather as a Force Multiplier" or allow the existence of HAARP and the IRI to be known by the public, all while we anxiously inched closer to the turn of a millennium, was proof to many that something else was going on here ... and it wasn't totally under control.

Thomas never used the term "chemtrails" in his story, but he did twice refer to them as "chemical contrails," and it would be only a matter of time before that phrase became a portmanteau. It was then adopted by other fringe science journalists, professional skeptics, and, most importantly in those early days, the famous radio host Art Bell, who shined a bright and constant light on the topic for years through his paranormal-themed syndicated talk show *Coast to Coast*.[7]

From there, the chemtrails conspiracy took off. Over the next two decades, it steadily increased in popularity both in the United States and abroad, and the motives ascribed to its conspirators expanded as well. In 1999, chemtrails were simply the sickly fingerprints of a clumsy government campaign to beat back global warming by spraying chemicals into the atmosphere. By 2019, depending on whom you talked to, they were the government's dispersal method of choice for all manner of geoengineering initiatives, sterilization efforts, mind-control campaigns, and bio- and chemical-weapons testing. Many even believe to this day that the respiratory illnesses allegedly caused by chemtrails aren't an unintended side effect; they are the entire point—part of a profit-driven Malthusian plot to reduce the population by weeding out the weak and the elderly while at the same time enriching pharmaceutical companies that are run by greedy CEOs with friends in high places.

It's tempting here to throw all these conspiratorially minded babies out with their chemically laced bathwater. But that would be a mistake. Because the government has done stuff just like this in the past. A lot. And not all that long ago.

---

[7] Bell had Thomas on numerous times over the years to discuss chemtrails and a variety of other conspiracy theories.

OPERATION LARGE AREA COVERAGE

UNLESS YOU'RE A CHEMIST, you're probably not familiar with zinc cadmium sulfide (ZnCdS). It's an odorless, insoluble, inorganic compound made of zinc sulfide and cadmium sulfide that was first developed as a paint pigment, and it's valued by science and industry primarily for its fluorescent properties. Today, it's used in everything from solar cells to dandruff shampoos. In the late 1950s, the US Army used it, programmatically, for a much less benign or follically related purpose.

From late 1957 through early 1958, in a series of dispersion tests called Operation Large Area Coverage (Operation LAC), the Army Chemical Corps sprayed ZnCdS over enormous swaths of the United States to simulate a biological or chemical attack. They used ZnCdS as a "simulant" for a few reasons: first, it fluoresced bright yellow under ultraviolet light, which made it easy to trace; second, its particle size, when aerosolized, closely mimicked the particle size of known biological agents; third, it was cheap; and fourth, it was believed to be of low toxicity with little bioavailability. In other words, it was easy to see, easy to measure, easy to get, and it wasn't going to kill anybody.

The goal of these dispersion tests was to determine whether coverage of a large area was possible at sufficient concentration for a biological attack to be effective (translation: lethal). From a borrowed US Air Force C-119, Operation LAC scientists released ZnCdS in varying quantities (from a few grams to hundreds of kilograms), with varying release windows (from seconds to hours), along a number of transcontinental flight paths that extended several hundred miles at the short end to 1,400 miles at the long end and covered virtually all of the continental United States east of the Rocky Mountains.

Right out of the gate, the tests bore troubling implications. The inaugural flight occurred on December 2, 1957. It went from South Dakota to International Falls, Minnesota. It was a fairly ordinary flight path covering 400 miles over which an extraordinary 5,000 pounds of ZnCdS was released. Almost immediately, the weather took a turn toward the northeast and an unexpected mass of cold air from Canada captured the majority of the particles carrying them nearly 1,200 miles straight up over Uncle Sam's oblivious northern neighbor. The Canadian government was not notified, it seems, that this was project was taking place. (Bioterrorism experts would later describe this as the largest experiment of its kind to that date.) A few months later, during a flight originating from Dugway Proving Ground in Utah, a similar weather event would drag a load of ZnCdS particles south out over the Gulf of Mexico. In both instances, the aerosolized particles that the Army Chemical Corps was trying to measure were pulled far away from the ground-based measuring stations meant to capture them. The weather had stripped the scientists of any sense of control over dispersion patterns, and it exposed just how dangerous a biological attack could be to people who weren't even the intended target.

Still, the tests were deemed a success. Operation LAC had provided the first proof of the viability of blanketing large parts of a country with biological weapons—a long-held belief among a lot of scientists and officers within the Army Chemical Corps. Long-held because these weren't the first tests of aerosolized biological weapon simulants. Rather, the Operation LAC flights were the culmination of dozens of prior, smaller tests all around the country that stretched back more than a decade and had their roots in a secret 1942 National Research Council (NRC) report on the threat of biological weapons that had been commissioned by the secretary of war just prior to American entry into World War II.

"The value of biological warfare will be a debatable question until it has been clearly proven or disproven by experience," the authors of the report wrote. "There is but one logical course to pursue, namely, to study the possibilities of such warfare from every angle, make every preparation for reducing its effectiveness, and thereby reduce the likelihood of its use."[8]

This rationale was reiterated fifty years later in the NRC's thorough evaluation of the army's ZnCdS dispersion tests. From the beginning, the United States' (official) biological weapons strategy was one of deterrence. This required a "thorough study and analysis of our vulnerability to overt and covert attack," recalled the authors of the 1997 report, as well as "extensive research and development to determine...the efficacy of our protective measures, and the tactical and strategic capability of various [biological weapons] agents and delivery systems."[9]

"Thorough study and analysis." "Extensive research and development." Two different ways to say "test, test, test, test, test."

From the end of World War II through the end of the 1960s when Richard Nixon halted the country's biological weapons program, the army conducted at least 160 such dispersion tests across 66 different locations. An army report submitted to the Senate Health Subcommittee in March 1977 cites 239 "open air" biowarfare tests in that period, of which those 166 were surely a part. The purpose of these tests, many of which would eventually lead to Operation Large Area Coverage, was to find answers to the army's more specific efficacy and efficiency questions.

What are the best simulants? How do particle clouds move over land? Or from sea to land? In cold weather versus warm weather? What happens with dispersion at various altitudes? What does it look like if particles are sprayed directly versus ejected from an explosive device? How do they spread in a forest? In a large city? Along the coast?

The Army Chemical Corps would get their answers to these questions.

---

[8] This quotation comes from a report by the War Bureau Consultants (WBC) Committee, which had been appointed by the National Academy of Sciences. The report would not be declassified until decades later, in 1988.

[9] From Toxicologic Assessment of the Army's Zinc Cadmium Sulfide Dispersion Tests, Appendix A, by the National Research Council (US) Subcommittee on Zinc Cadmium Sulfide. (1997)

In addition to zinc cadmium sulfide, they found organic bacteria such as *Serratia marcescens*, *Bacillus globigii*, *Bacillus subtilis*, and *Aspergillus fumigatus* were physically similar enough to their weaponized counterparts to stand in as simulants and were considered nontoxic or nonpathogenic enough to use in quantities sufficient for testing. The organic and inorganic compounds were often used together: sometimes mixed into one cocktail, other times dispersed simultaneously.

In September 1950, less than three months after the US officially entered the Korean War, the army staged at least six simulated attacks on San Francisco as part of Operation Moby Dick. Over a seven-day period, they shot a slurry of *S. marcescens* and *B. globigii* into the famous San Francisco fog bank through giant hoses aboard a ship sailing just beyond the Golden Gate Bridge, hoping to figure out whether "a successful [biological warfare] attack on this area can be launched from the sea."[10] (They concluded it was feasible.)

In spring 1952, five experiments off the coast of South Carolina and Georgia called Operation Dew sought to determine whether clouds bearing biowarfare agents could easily disperse across hundreds of miles if the weather was right.

In spring 1953, Operation White-Horse was a series of twelve tests off the coast of the Florida panhandle, using the same bacterial combination as the San Francisco experiments in concert with ZnCdS, to see what happens to an "aerosol cloud ... formed at sea level" as it makes its way onshore.

Experiments occurred in Minnesota beginning in 1953 as well, including one that directed an aerosol cloud at a school. The cloud was so dense that it was actually visible inside the school. Around the same time or shortly after, the army conducted multiple experiments in Saint Louis, Missouri, spraying ZnCdS from motorized blowers on high rooftops in low-income areas.

---

[10] Presumably by Chinese or North Korean military vessels.

In the 1960s, as Cold War paranoia reached fever pitch, the tests got even more frightening. In 1965, agents from the Special Operations Division at Fort Detrick, which was home to the country's bioweapons program and run by the Army Chemical Corps, spread *S. marcescens* throughout Washington DC's National Airport.[11] In 1966, for "A Study of the Vulnerability of Subway Passengers in New York City to Covert Attack with Biological Agents," a test whose name leaves nothing to the imagination, army scientists sent *S. marcescens* and *B. subtilis* through the New York subway system by packing trillions of the microbes into lightbulbs, dropping them onto the tracks from between moving subway cars, then waiting for the next train to roar past and carry the invisible particles with it. "It went quite well through the subway system," a retired army scientist named Charles Senseney testified to a congressional subcommittee in 1975. "We started down around 14th Street and sampled up as far as about 58th Street and there [was] quite a bit of aerosol all along the way." Even more startling, New York City officials were completely unaware of the studies taking place, quite literally, right under their feet.

> **In the 1960s, as Cold War paranoia reached fever pitch, the tests got even more frightening.**

There is, of course, more. Much more. Some of it emerged from army records acquired through Freedom of Information Act (FOIA) requests in the early 1990s.[12] For instance, many more of these dispersion tests than just the two that bookended Operation LAC spread beyond the control or the expectations of the Army Chemical Corps. Between 1951 and 1956, no fewer than thirty-five tests conducted at the Dugway Proving Ground may

---

[11] National Airport is barely three miles, as the crow flies, from both the White House and the Capitol Building.

[12] It's not hard to imagine that William Thomas was well-acquainted with the existence of these documents prior to his chemtrails article in early 1999.

have spread beyond the designated testing area. In two separate instances at Dugway, one in 1962 and one in 1968, the army dropped more than a ton of the nerve agent VX. Only 4 percent of the VX in the 1962 test hit the mark. In 1968, the army did a little better, but still as much as half of the dispersant spread outside the testing ground. And the next day local ranchers reported more than 6,000 sheep turning up dead, for which the army paid $1 million in restitution without acknowledging responsibility. All told, the army dropped nearly 500,000 pounds of VX at the Dugway Proving Ground and conducted 328 "open air germ warfare tests" between 1949 and 1986.

This is what we know from the documents that the US government was willing to declassify after the end of the Cold War or that journalists have been able to extract through FOIA requests. And still, much remains classified, redacted, and unknown. As troubling as it is to admit, the public may never know the full extent of these biowarfare experiments—which is a big part of the reason that the chemtrails conspiracy theory persists, just like those thick, crisscrossing contrails its proponents don't trust. *Maybe*, they would conjecture, *the experiments never ended*.

THE SAND IN
THE PEARL

THERE ARE OTHER, related explanations for the theory's persistence. Cloud seeding, for example. Scientists theorized about the ability to modify the weather and increase precipitation all the way back in the late nineteenth century. In the mid-1940s, two scientists from General Electric proved it was possible. In two separate sets of experiments, one using dry ice and the other silver iodide, they were able to increase the number of particles around which water vapor in a cloud could condense and, thus, form a

13

greater concentration of raindrops or ice crystals within the cloud. In the decades since then, countries all over the world have been experimenting with and actively implementing cloud-seeding programs to combat drought, to dissipate fog around airports, to reduce the size of hailstones that develop in thunderclouds, to weaken hurricanes, and to increase snowfall around ski resorts.[13]

In addition, researchers are currently studying the potential of solar geoengineering, called albedo modification, to reflect the sun's rays back into space and reduce greenhouse gases. A team of scientists in the School of Engineering and Applied Sciences at Harvard University is well into the experiment design phase. In language reminiscent of the patent issued to Hughes Aircraft Company back in the early '90s that William Thomas cited, they announced on an undated page of their website that they are "actively developing proposals for field experiments" that would involve "add[ing] materials to the Earth's atmosphere to reflect a bit more sunlight back to space." In other words, they're trying to seed the clouds. Or more to the point, spray stuff in the sky.

Where this becomes problematic for the more suspiciously minded is in the debate over the effectiveness of cloud seeding. The effects appear to be temporary. Precipitation increases tend to be minor. And the results, at least in the case of hurricane experiments, have shown to be dangerously unpredictable. There are also the physical properties of silver iodide to consider. It is a bright yellow nonorganic compound, not unlike zinc cadmium sulfide, that has been listed as a priority pollutant by the Environmental Protection Agency since the passage of the Clean Water Act in 1977. And according to chemical companies that manufacture the stuff, it is known to cause skin and eye irritation, runny nose, headaches, and respiratory issues for those who come in contact with it. Sound familiar?

---

[13] The Chinese government even used cloud seeding prior to the 2008 Olympics in Beijing in order to stave off rain for the three weeks during which the games were held.

When you add that to all the things we know today about the army's open-air dispersion tests that even the government didn't know back then, the chemtrails picture gets even clearer—to the conspiracy theorist, at least. We know, for instance, that a significant number of the simulants the army believed were benign can, in fact, be harmful to people with weakened or compromised immune systems.

A British study in the late 1980s found a number of *B. subtilis* infections among cancer patients, including septicemia and fatal cases of pneumonia and bacteremia. The bacterium also produces a toxic enzyme (of low virulence) called subtilisin that has caused skin irritation and respiratory problems for people who are allergic. The bacteria's cousin *B. globigii* has similarly been reclassified as a human pathogen for its role in food poisoning and as an agent of typically nonfatal infections in hospital patients who have undergone surgical procedures or have been catheterized for extended periods.

S. marcescens, which turns an alarmingly creepy blood red when a colony of the bacteria forms, has also been reclassified in the last forty years as an "opportunistic pathogen." It isn't responsible for many primary infections in healthy people, but among the very young, very old, and immunocompromised, it is a particular threat, especially in a hospital setting. *S. marcescens* is now understood to cause pneumonia, urinary tract infections, lower respiratory tract infections, bloodstream infections, and even meningitis.

In 1950, in the months after Operation Moby Dick, *S. marcescens* sickened at least ten people with pneumonia symptoms in the San Francisco area—where the presence of the bacteria was exceedingly rare—and it killed a man named Edward Nevin who was recuperating from prostate cancer surgery at a San Francisco hospital, only to contract a nasty UTI that contained the bacteria that eventually spread to his heart. Thirty years later, Nevin's family sued the federal government for wrongful death. "We have been motivated by the horrible specter of the Government conducting potentially fatal tests on an uninformed public," Nevin's grandson, a law-yer, said at the time. The family's suit failed. On appeal, the Ninth Circuit Court affirmed that the government wasn't liable for negligence, in large part because the legality of the army's tests could not be subject to judicial review since it "would likely impair the effective administration of the government programs believed to be vital to the defense of the United States at the time that they are conducted." Basically, according to the American judicial sys-tem, the government can get away with sickening and even killing you if they *think* they're protecting a sufficiently large number of your fellow citizens. (If you're the Nevin family, that probably doesn't feel much like justice.)

It's an even scarier story with *Aspergillus fumigatus*. We breathe in this airborne fungus all the time, and if our immune systems are healthy, we expel the spores with no problem, which is probably why it was considered a viable nontoxic candidate as a bioweapons simulant in the 1950s and '60s. In recent decades, however, as more and more people have become immuno-compromised or immunosuppressed in the course of treating other illnesses, *A. fumigatus* has been responsible for a massive spike in invasive aspergil-losis, an infection caused by the fungus. A spike so great that, in a journal article in the spring of 1999, one of the world's foremost experts on *A. fumi-gatus*, Professor Jean-Paul Latgé of the Pasteur Institute in Paris, called it "the most common mold infection worldwide" and found that it occurred in at least 10 percent of leukemia patients, heart-and-lung transplant patients, blood disorder patients, and increasingly at the time, AIDS patients.

Oh, the sickening irony! These four microorganisms, now understood to be pathogenic, were sprayed by the literal ton on dozens of occasions over numerous American towns and cities to simulate the spread of *known* deadly pathogens so that we might be better equipped to protect ourselves in the event of an actual biological weapons attack. All of this was done without the knowledge or consent of the people who lived in the affected areas, the consequences from which the government was immune, but the weak and infirm sadly were not.

These, we know today, are incontrovertible facts. We also know that the army's dispersion tests were kept secret for more than twenty-five years. We know that city officials across the country (and in Canada) were kept in the dark about them. Even when they were consulted, as was the case with the dispersion tests in Minneapolis in 1952, we know it was only to feed them misinformation in the event that concerned citizens reported seeing government trucks, roof-mounted blowers, buzzing gray boxes on street corners, and clouds of vapor circulating through the city at all hours of the day and night. Army officials were creating a smokescreen for their tests—one that turned out to be a story about *actual* smokescreens. They told Minneapolis officials that they were trying to "measure ability to lay smoke screens about the city" as a defensive measure against Soviet nuclear attack. It was a story that would get picked up by the *Minneapolis Tribune* in January of the following year, and by a number of other regional newspapers thereafter, which had the desired effect of almost immediately quieting public concern about all the mysterious activity and letting the army get back to their spraying, unbothered.

All these facts—from cloud seeding with silver iodide to plans for solar geoengineering experiments, from poorly controlled dispersal tests to poorly understood bacterial pathogens—are the proverbial grains of sand at the center of the pearl that is the chemtrails conspiracy theory. They are the bits of hard, aggravating truth that the innumerable layers of cognitively biased claims, logical leaps, faulty assumptions, and hasty conclusions wrapped themselves around until enough of them had coalesced to form something smooth and shiny and manipulable. They are what gives the chemtrails theory its tangibility and object permanence. You can deny concerns about population control. You can disprove accusations about mind control. But you can't simply dismiss claims about bioweapons testing or geoengineering or the sudden onset of respiratory problems, because those things all really happened! For decades, governments have tried to mess with the weather. For years and years, the American government has

17

sprayed thousands of pounds of pathogenic bacteria and fungi into the sky and didn't tell anybody. A lie by omission if there ever was one.

Any good-faith debate about the existence of chemtrails must reckon with the truth of these past (and current) actions. Any honest attempt to debunk this conspiracy theory once and for all has to begin with understanding that these facts comprise the foundation of distrust in government upon which the entire theory is constructed—and it's a mighty sturdy foundation if you ask us. Indeed, the blueprint for every successful conspiracy theory has exactly this kind of foundation. Put another way, there is no such thing as a pearl with a hollow core. There are always grains of sand at the center. There is always some truth.

HIV AND LYME DISEASE

SOMETIMES THAT TRUTH IS SHARED across different theories. When you spend as much time as we do researching conspiracies, you come to learn that a lot of conspiracy theories share DNA. This is certainly the case with chemtrails and the theories behind the origins of human immunodeficiency virus (HIV) and Lyme disease.

It has been postulated for decades, by a surprisingly large percentage of the population, that HIV was created as a biological warfare agent in an American laboratory—likely the US military's bioweapons labs at Fort Detrick. Some have gone so far as to assert that the virus was made for the purpose of the mass extinction of Black Americans and Africans worldwide. This theory caught on quickly and found immediate support within both communities, including from prominent cultural figures such as Will Smith, Bill Cosby, Louis Farrakhan, Reverend Jeremiah Wright, and the

Kenyan ecologist Wangari Maathai, who, in 2004, became the first African woman to win the Nobel Peace Prize.[14] Polling throughout the United States over the last thirty-plus years consistently shows that 40 to 50 percent of people believe HIV is a man-made virus, concocted either on purpose in a government lab or by accident from an experiment that got out of control. Fully a quarter of respondents believe that HIV was designed to deliberately affect Black people and/or wipe them off the planet.

The numbers are similar when Black South Africans are polled, though their conspiratorial narrative is slightly different and more personal. By the mid-2000s, the most popular theory was that HIV was created by the US government in cooperation with Dr. Wouter Basson, the head of the apartheid government's biological weapons program. Codenamed Project Coast, the program just happened to get going in the same years that the first official cases of HIV and AIDS were being clinically observed in the United States. Basson was a particular target of conspiracy theorists because he had been tried a few years earlier in a South African court on sixty-seven different charges—including multiple murders, conspiracy, and drug manufacturing—related to his work developing covert bioweapons that had been turned against freedom fighters and political opponents in South Africa and neighboring countries. Nicknamed "Dr. Death" by the South African press during the trial, which stretched from 1999 to 2002, Basson was eventually acquitted of all charges. Which might make you wonder: *How does a guy called Dr. Death walk away scot-free from charges that include 229 murders without a little help from his gray flannel–suited friends?*

Needless to say, the HIV bioweapons theory has a number of variations, and just like with chemtrails theories, all of them have been sticky. And they owe their stickiness to very similar grains of sand at the center of the different pearls. In this case, it's not just that these governments have a

---

[14] Maathai said, in a press conference held in Nairobi the day after receiving the Nobel Prize, that "the HIV virus is created by a scientist for biological warfare. Why has there been so much secrecy about AIDS? When you ask where did the virus come from, it raises a lot of flags."

long history of conducting bioweapons research and clandestine field testing—some of it in high-density, low-income urban areas that were home to predominantly Black residents, as was the case in Saint Louis[15]—but that they also have a history of abject racism and of targeting the Black community with their intelligence and law enforcement agencies.

In the United States, beginning in 1932, poor Black sharecroppers from Tuskegee, Alabama, were the unwitting subjects of a government syphilis study that lasted the better part of forty years and killed 128 of the 600 men enrolled in the study. In the infamous MKUltra program of the 1960s, Blacks were overwhelmingly targeted by the CIA for its LSD experiments. (We'll talk about these actual conspiracies in more detail in the next chapter.) And during the same period, as part of the FBI's wide-ranging counterintelligence program, COINTELPRO, Black activists were surveilled, Black organizations were infiltrated, and many were incited to violence and murder in the course of the FBI's activities. (We'll talk more about COINTELPRO in chapter 3.)

Imagine being a Black American in the 1980s. You hear there is an awful new disease that has appeared basically out of nowhere, and it's killing Black people in disproportionate numbers. No one in the government or the medical establishment can tell you what it is exactly, or where it came from, or how to cure it. Knowing the history of your government's actions and attitudes toward the Black community, would you be inclined to believe them? Or would you maybe ask yourself, *what do they really know about this thing and why aren't they telling us?* It's a question that many Black Americans have asked themselves over the last forty years. And, according to historical survey data, many people asking themselves this question ultimately conclude *the government must be in on it.*

---

[15] In one set of tests, the Army Chemical Corps mounted motorized blowers atop the roof of a low-income high-rise building. In army documents from the period, the testing area was described as "a densely populated slum district."

With Lyme disease, it's America's bioweapons history combined with the disease's emergence from seemingly out of nowhere that bonds it with chemtrails and HIV as an object of conspiratorial theorizing. The first known outbreak of what came to

According to historical survey data, many people asking themselves this question ultimately conclude *the government must be in on it.*

be called Lyme disease occurred in July 1975 in the town of Old Lyme, Connecticut, on the northern shore of the Long Island Sound. Thirty-nine kids and twelve adults complained of the strange and sudden onset of headaches, skin rashes, and swollen joints. Doctors from Yale were immediately brought in by the Connecticut Health Department to examine everyone. Their diagnosis was a form of juvenile rheumatoid arthritis that they dubbed "Lyme arthritis." It wouldn't be for another couple of years that scientists would be able to link the symptoms of the residents of Old Lyme to deer tick bites. And it would be another couple of years after that until a scientist from the National Institutes of Health (NIH) named Willy Burgdorfer would finally discover the bacterium that was responsible for the illness, at which point Lyme arthritis officially became Lyme *disease.*

Named after Burgdorfer, who was one of the world's leading experts in tick-borne diseases like relapsing fever and Rocky Mountain spotted fever, *Borrelia burgdorferi* is a spiral-shaped bacterium that attacks the central nervous system and wreaks havoc in all sorts of unpredictable ways. Some people suffer skin irritation and flulike symptoms and recover in a week or so with a regimen of antibiotics; others get laid out with serious cardiac afflictions and respiratory problems that can last a long time and ruin their quality of life. Sounds a lot like the health problems described by chemtrail proponents, doesn't it?

Here's where it gets crazy. Ten miles directly across the Long Island Sound from Old Lyme is Plum Island. Today, Plum Island is home to the Plum Island Animal Disease Center (PIADC). Run by the Department of Agriculture, the mission of the PIADC is to study foreign animal diseases that infect livestock and threaten the food supply. But in 1952, just as the Cold War was beginning to heat up, the island was run by the US Army. And wouldn't you know it, our old friends from the Army Chemical Corps were there too. They were conducting anti-animal biowarfare research out of a lab in Building 257 aimed at disrupting the Soviet Union's national food supply. The Chemical Corps operated at Plum Island for only a short time, however. In July 1954, ownership of the island transferred to the Department of Agriculture (USDA). The USDA took over the biowarfare research from that point. They continued the work on anti-animal pathogens until the official termination of the American bioweapons program under Nixon in 1969, just six short years before the first recorded Lyme disease outbreak right across the sound.

Is it possible that the government was trying to weaponize deer ticks on Plum Island? Why not? Between 1954 and 1956, the Chemical Corps had already conducted at least four separate tests involving the dispersal of other types of arthropods and insects to evaluate their viability as vectors for the spread of disease. In 1954, they successfully dropped a few hundred thousand tropical rat fleas over Dugway Proving Ground as part of Operation Big Itch. In 1955, it was 300,000 mosquitos in Georgia as part of Operation Big Buzz. In 1956, it was even more mosquitos, this time over residential and urban areas of Savannah, Georgia, as part of Operation Drop Kick and Operation May Day. And of course, we already know that ticks naturally carry a number of different febrile illnesses.

Accepting that as a possibility, could some number of these weaponized ticks have escaped containment from Building 257 in the summer of 1975 and made the jump over to Old Lyme? Put it this way: Plum Island is home to colonies of numerous species of birds, which are known to carry ticks and fly between the island and the shore on a regular basis. Deer have been known to swim surprisingly long distances, particularly those native to wooded coastal areas dotted with island chains. And deer ticks, well, they can be submerged in water for up to three days and survive with little problem.

Look at what we have here now. Three conspiracy theories, spanning three decades, that share connections to the Army Chemical Corps and Cold War bioweapons programs, to dispersal tests and experiments that got out of control, and to the sudden appearance of seemingly inexplicable events that caused all sorts of health problems.

What in the name of William Thomas is going on here?!

CLEARING THE AIR

THE REALITY IS THIS: contrails, HIV, and Lyme disease have very straight-forward scientific and sociological explanations.

Persistent contrails have always existed. Those earliest photos from the 1940s actually show crisscrossing patterns of persistent contrails left behind by dogfighting military aircraft in both the Pacific and European theaters of World War II.

There are more of these contrails today because there are more airplanes in the sky. In the thirty years between the end of the US bioweapons program in 1969 and the publication of Will Thomas's Environment News Service article in 1999, the number of commercial air passengers increased 500 percent. It tripled again over the next twenty years. In 2019, commercial airlines flew nearly 4.4 billion passengers worldwide. That's more than half the planet!

There are more crisscrossing contrails today because with more aircraft in the sky, the air corridors within which planes are allowed to fly—to take off and land, in particular—are increasingly narrow and strictly enforced. This is due to a combination of restricted military airspace; lower altitude airspace reserved for smaller, single-engine aircraft; seasonal migratory bird flyways that pose increased risks for bird strikes; and noise reduction ordinances in neighborhoods surrounding airports. Simply put, there are only so many patches of sky that large planes are allowed to fly through. So when the temperature, humidity, and altitude are right in one of those corridors, what you're going to get is a three-dimensional checkerboard made of blue sky and white contrails.

In the case of HIV, the virus did not appear out of nowhere. In what is called a zoonotic event in epidemiology,[16] it jumped from Central African chimpanzees that were carrying the related simian immunodeficiency virus (SIV). Transmission likely occurred as a result of chimpanzees being hunted for food by humans who came into contact with the chimps' infected blood while butchering them. According to the CDC, studies appear to show that the virus may have jumped to humans as far back as the late nineteenth century, nearly a hundred years before it showed up in hospital patients in the United States.

The fact that the virus seemed to be targeting particular groups was a classic case of correlation instead of causation. Black people were not a target. Africans were not a target. Gays were not a target. There were no "targets" at all. The entire world's population was, and is, at risk for the disease, and the degree of risk is defined not by race or sexual orientation but by behavior. Specifically, intravenous drug use and high-risk sexual practices. Those were, and continue to be, the primary modes of disease transmission.

---

[16] While infrequent, zoonotic events are not uncommon. In the twenty-first century alone, they have been responsible for outbreaks of Ebola, Rift Valley fever, SARS, MERS, swine flu, bird flu, Zika virus, and COVID-19.

It's a similar story with Lyme disease. Populations of deer ticks around Plum Island did not suddenly become superaggressive hosts of *B. burgdorferi* and start biting Connecticut schoolchildren and their parents. Museum specimens collected on Long Island in the 1940s, well before the biowarfare lab in Building 257 was opened, were found to be infected with the bacteria. And it wasn't just deer ticks that carried it. Museum specimens of mice from Cape Cod dating back to 1896 were positive for *B. burgdorferi* as well. Its origins also aren't modern or North American. Evidence of Lyme disease was found in the preserved cadaver of Oetzi, the famous 5,300-year-old Tyrolean iceman, who was unearthed in the Italian Alps in 1991. In 2008, a team of researchers from the University of Bath discovered that *B. burgdorferi* was much older than that still, dating back to before the last ice age.

What, then, explains the explosion of Lyme disease cases beginning in the mid-1970s? The disease-causing bacteria may be prehistoric, and there may have been misdiagnosed cases dating back decades, if not centuries, but nowhere in the history books has there been discussion of an unexplained epidemic with symptoms like those common to Lyme disease.

The answer to that question has two parts. The first has to do with reforestation. Much of the forest in the greater New England region had been clear-cut in the eighteenth and nineteenth centuries to make room for farming, which was the principal means of subsistence prior to industrialization. This had the effect of nearly wiping out the white-tailed deer population, which is the primary host of deer ticks. As farming moved west in the twentieth century, however, the trees grew back and the white-tailed deer population did too. With a vengeance. It exploded, and with it the deer tick population.

Interestingly, the second part of the answer is also part of the answer to questions about contrails and HIV: It's *deforestation*. It's urban and suburban sprawl. It's people. *Us.* We are the masters of our own misery, just as we are the gods of our own delusions.

21ST CENTURY ZOONOTIC DISEASES

A zoonotic event occurs when a pathogen (virus, bacteria, parasite, etc.) passes, or "jumps", from its animal host to humans, making them ill. These infections are then called zoonotic diseases. Typically, transmission occurs in one of a small handful of ways: direct contact with animal blood, saliva or waste, as with HIV; being bitten, as with ticks and Lyme disease or mosquitos and malaria; indirect contact with areas where animals live or travel, like barns or topsoil; contaminated food or water, like with *E. coli*. This century alone, there have already been several zoonotic diseases either emerge for the first time or have renewed outbreaks.

DISEASE	SPECIES ORIGIN	GEOGRAPHIC ORIGIN	DISCOVERY DATE	21ST CENTURY OUTBREAK DATES	CASES/ DEATHS
EBOLA*	Fruit bats	Guinea, Sierra Leone, Liberia	1976	Dec 2013 – Jan 2016	28,610/ 11,308
RIFT VALLEY FEVER**	Livestock	Kenya, Somalia, Tanzania	1930	Nov 2006 – May 2007	1,062/ 394
SARS (Severe Acute Respiratory Syndrome)	Horseshoe bats; masked palm civets	China	2002	Nov 2002 – Jul 2003	8,096/ 774

In the decades after World War II, the suburban building boom touched every corner of the country, including Long Island and Connecticut. Large homes, subdivisions, entire towns were carved out of the newly regrown forest, bringing more and more people into contact with an out-of-control deer population that, we know now, was infested with Lyme disease—carrying ticks. It was only a matter of time before an explosion of people turned an explosion of white-tailed deer into an explosion of deer ticks into an

DISEASE	SPECIES ORIGIN	GEOGRAPHIC ORIGIN	DISCOVERY DATE	21ST CENTURY OUTBREAK DATES	CASES/DEATHS
MERS (Middle East Respiratory Syndrome)	Bats; camels	Saudi Arabia	2012	Apr 2012 – Oct 2021	2,578/888
SWINE FLU	Pigs	Mexico	2008/09	Jun 2009 – Aug 2010	700 million -1.4 billion/ 284,500
AVIAN FLU*** (H7N9)	Geese; Poultry; Wild birds	China	2013	Mar 2013 – Dec 2017	1,565/610
ZIKA VIRUS	Mosquitos; monkeys	Uganda	1947	Apr 2015 – Nov 2016	millions/ almost no deaths****
COVID-19	Bats	China	2019	Dec 2019 – Present	~300 million/ ~5.5 million^^

*   There have been approximately two dozen outbreaks since Ebola's discovery, more than fifteen of them this century. The outbreak in 2013-16 in West Africa was the largest and deadliest.

**   Like Ebola, there have been multiple RVF outbreaks all across the African continent since 2000. The 2006 outbreak was the largest and most widespread.

*** There are many, many avian flu strains, dating back to the late 1870s. The H7N9 virus is the most recent variant that has epidemiologists the most concerned about its potential to become pandemic.

**** Because of the mildness of Zika symptoms and the almost negligible death toll, officials believe cases were wildly underreported. However, in Brazil, where the global outbreak began in 2015, 3,500 cases of microcephaly in newborns were reported.

^^   These figures were accurate as of Jan 17, 2022.

explosion of Lyme disease cases. That it didn't happen until 1975 is purely a product of chance.

Sprawl is also why 90 percent of Americans today live within an hour of a decent-size airport. (That figure is 77 percent in the United Kingdom.) Is it any wonder we're seeing more intersecting contrails, then? We're all living within sight or earshot of an airport's traffic pattern, in a time when approximately 100,000 flights take off and land every day.

Yet with the jump and spread of HIV, it wasn't the sprawl of the population on the African continent outward that was the issue; according to some evolutionary virologists, it was the concentration of the population into cities during the colonial period of the late nineteenth and early twentieth centuries. The arrival of white Europeans and colonial administration brought a tendency toward centralization. It brought new, different sexual mores. It brought prostitution and increased promiscuity. It brought syphilis and other genital ulcer diseases that increased the transmissibility of SIV and the earliest strains of HIV by as much as 40 percent. This, they argue, set the virus on its way across Africa over the next fifty years and then out into the rest of the world in the 1970s and '80s.

THE LIE WITHIN THE LIE WITHIN THE LIE

THE GOVERNMENT has not made explanations like these particularly compelling to most conspiracy theorists. The confirmation bias of a skeptic who has turned into a cynic is often too strong to overcome. Every statement of fact produces a healthy dose of what-about-ism.

Sure, there are more planes in the sky than ever, but what about that congressman who introduced legislation to stop the use of chemtrails?[17]

Yeah, OK, HIV jumped from chimps to humans, but what about COVID-19? It jumped from species to species, too, but now they're also saying it came from a government lab.

---

[17] In 2001, Rep. Dennis Kucinich sponsored a bill on the floor of the House of Representatives, titled the Space Preservation Act, in which he sought to ban all space-based weapons systems, including "chemtrails."

I get it; the deer tick bacterium has been around for hundreds of thousands of years, but what about that bipartisan amendment demanding an investigation by the Pentagon into whether the military was weaponizing ticks during the Cold War?[18]

That's what it's like trying to get to the bottom of a conspiracy theory. You've got the pearl in your hand, you think you've got it under control, but when you push on a spot, the pearl just starts to spin. And the more you push, the more it spins. That's because, more often than not, the institutions providing the information that would otherwise explain away a conspiracy theory like chemtrails or the origins of HIV and Lyme disease are the institutions at the heart of the distrust that gave those theories life in the first place.

The government lied about its bioweapons testing program. Then when they got found out, they lied about why they lied. And even then they still didn't get to the *real lie.*

The government lied about its bioweapons testing program. Then when they got found out, they lied about why they lied.

In the 1950s, the army told cities that they were testing the ability to create smokescreens to defend cities against Soviet nuclear attacks. This was a lie. When programs like Operation LAC were uncovered in the 1970s, the government admitted that what they were really doing was testing to see how biowarfare agents would spread across America's towns and cities in the event of a Soviet biological or chemical attack. They wanted to know what the most effective methods of dispersal were so they could gauge whether the US was prepared or could be protected. This, too, was a lie. In the NRC review of

---

[18] In 2019, Rep. Christopher Smith from New Jersey introduced an amendment to a defense authorization bill requiring the Department of Defense to reveal whether they did bioweapons research on ticks and other insects between 1950 and 1975. The amendment was cosponsored by a Democrat from Minnesota and a Republican from Maryland—two states intimately familiar with the legacy of the American bioweapons program.

the army's ZnCdS usage, conducted in the 1990s, it's clear that these tests quickly became offensive in nature. A number of cities had been selected for dispersion tests because of their geographic, topographic, and demographic similarities to Soviet cities on American military target lists. The US government was conducting simulations and test runs on its own people as stand-ins for the Soviets. With bioagents of unknown toxicity. All without the people's knowledge or consent.

In fairness to the government, it's reasonable to conjecture that the option of informed consent was off the table from the start. To go public with the experiments would have exposed the current state of US bioweapons research, while also signaling (rightly or wrongly) possible plans for a future biowarfare attack to a notoriously paranoid USSR. Additionally, elected officials complicit in these activities would have considered a public admission political suicide. It's one thing to talk about doing hard things for the greater good in private conversations with donors and colleagues,[19] but convincing the American public to agree to this level of uncontrolled exposure is an altogether different, more challenging conversation. The acronym NIMBY—Not In My Backyard—may not have been coined until 1980, but politicians have long been aware of, and highly sensitive to, the consequences of this behavioral tendency.

But this touches only obliquely on the bigger issue with admitting to the existence of these tests or seeking consent from the public before they're conducted. To do so would have been to admit, just as tensions on the Korean Peninsula were exploding into war and postwar diplomatic relations with the USSR had turned officially frosty, that the government had no idea about any of this stuff. Of course, no government in their right mind would ever admit such a thing. And frankly, the general public doesn't want to hear it. Nobody wants to believe that the people responsible for their safety and security, especially in a country that was well on its way

---

[19] We'll talk more about the implications of these kinds of conversations in chapter 8, which covers lobbying.

to becoming the most powerful nation in the history of human civilization, was in the dark.

Except they were. Factions of government agencies acted with little to no oversight, meaning that the larger government—Congress, the judiciary, and so on—was basically clueless, effectively blind. And tests like Operation LAC, run by the Army Chemical Corps out of a dedicated facility like Fort Detrick, were the government's systematic effort to learn how to see.

That is the lie within the lie within the lie—one that we will see, again and again as this book goes along, is at the heart of many proven government conspiracies. And our unwillingness or inability to own up to that fact is why conspiracy theories like chemtrails, HIV, and Lyme disease continue to proliferate, spinning around and around, collecting additional layers of shiny detail faster and faster, the more we try to break them apart.

CHAPTER TWO

HUMAN EXPERIMENTATION

IT'S APRIL 1991 AND A MYSTERIOUS FLYER HAS BEGUN TO APPEAR IN THE CORRIDORS of apartment buildings and the windows of convenience stores all over New York City. Someone has even hired an army of kids to hand them out on street corners in Brooklyn, the Bronx, and Harlem.

ATTENTION!!! ATTENTION!!! ATTENTION!!!
50 CENT SODAS
BLACKS AND MINORITY GROUPS
DID YOU SEE (T.V. SHOW) 20/20???
PLEASE BE ADVISE, "Top Pop" & "Tropical Fantasy" .50 sodas are being manufactured by the Klu..Klux..Klan. Sodas contain stimulants to sterilize the black man, and who knows what else!!!! They are only put in stores in Harlem and minority areas. You won't find them down town .... Look around ....
YOU HAVE BEEN WARNED
PLEASE SAVE THE CHILDREN

Top Pop and Tropical Fantasy, along with a third brand called A-Treat, are low-cost sodas often sold in convenience stores located in densely populated, traditionally nonwhite urban areas. If you've never heard of these sodas, there's a reason. They don't run big advertising campaigns. There are no billboards or radio spots or placards on the roofs of taxicabs. In 1991, before Google or social media, the only way you'd ever have known these sodas existed was if you lived in a neighborhood where they were sold and saw them on store shelves with your own eyes.

This makes the so-called fifty-cent sodas an ideal target for a conspiracy like the one described on these flyers. Coca-Cola and Pepsi are sold everywhere. So are 7Up, Dr Pepper, and A&W Root Beer. You can find these brands on store shelves in every town in America, and in many towns all over the world. So if you're in the Ku Klux Klan and you're targeting the Black community, you'd be risking a lot of collateral damage among your own people by poisoning a widely popular drink. The specificity of the detail that it was *only* fifty-cent sodas being poisoned was evidence to many Black New Yorkers that they were being singled out . . . again.[1]

This was not an original story. In the mid-1980s, a story began to circulate in the Black community that the KKK was the true owner of the fried-chicken restaurant chain, Church's Chicken, and they were contaminating the chicken in order to sterilize Black men. Just like the fifty-cent sodas, Church's franchises were located "primarily in neighborhoods with high concentrations of Blacks" and they did very little advertising compared to their competition. Additionally, Church's menu carried many staples based on traditional southern Black cuisine. "[It] boasts a wide selection of foods not unlike those available at a soul food restaurant," as folklorist Patricia Turner put it in a 1987 article about the Church's conspiracy theory.

---

[1]   There were a few different versions of the flyer that circulated around New York City. Some included A-Treat, some didn't.

"If a white supremacist organization were going to use a fast food chain to infiltrate the black community, Church's would be 'made to order.'"[2]

It can take years to correct such contamination and sterilization theories, especially when, as was the case with these rumors, no one was able to track down the original source of the allegations. Whoever crafted this lie was also clever to cite reputable news magazine shows—*20/20* and *60 Minutes*, respectively—as proof of their claims. Today, a 30-second internet search could easily prove that the stories didn't exist, but at the time it was hard to verify such a fact. In the 1980s and '90s, it required a lot more sleuthing that no one outside the founders of Church's Chicken or the bottlers of Tropical Fantasy felt the need to do.

Sales of the fifty-cent sodas plummeted by 70 percent. It would take a massive PR campaign that included New York City's first Black mayor, David Dinkins, drinking a bottle of soda on television to finally turn sales around by 1991. With Church's Chicken, it wasn't until the larger Popeyes chain took them over that the story started to fade into the background.[3]

Still, neither of the conspiracy theories has fully gone away. In 2000, on a track titled "One," the New York rapper Ghostface Killah has a line specifically referencing this theory. In a 2012 post for NewsOne about the Church's Chicken claims, the writer concluded her piece by saying, "to this day, I—and I hang my head down in shame as I write this—will not allow any of my male family members to consume Church's Fried Chicken!"

These sterilization conspiracy theories have had staying power in the Black community for a very simple reason: they are based in conspiracy

---

[2] Patricia A. Turner, "Church's Fried Chicken and The Klan: A Rhetorical Analysis of Rumor in the Black Community," *Western Folklore* 46, no. 4 (1987): 294–306.

[3] A third, related conspiracy theory about Snapple popped up a year after the Tropical Fantasy flyers. In 1992, whispers began to emerge that Snapple had ties to the Ku Klux Klan. The ship on the label of Snapple bottles was a slave ship, theorists claimed, and the encircled K next to it was a symbol for the KKK. In reality the ship was a drawing from the Boston Tea Party, and the K denoted that Snapple beverages were kosher—a point of importance to the three Jewish co-founders, who, in responding to rumors a year later in an interview with MTV, asked the obvious question that helped to put things to rest: "How could three Jewish boys from Brooklyn support the Ku Klux Klan?"

fact. There is real history that lends them the veneer of credibility, and it goes beyond the widely known racism of the Ku Klux Klan and their nationalist desires for racial purity. It is today well established that the eugenics movement of the early twentieth century influenced government policies and inspired shadowy research programs that disproportionately affected the health, well-being, and very existence of historically disadvantaged populations—foremost among them, Black men.

PLATO, GALTON, AND THE (UN)NATURAL SELECTION OF EUGENICS

A TERM DERIVED FROM ANCIENT GREEK, meaning "well born" or "of noble stock," eugenics is technically "the study of how to arrange reproduction within a human population to increase the occurrence of heritable characteristics regarded as desirable." As it was initially conceived, eugenics was often discussed in a positive way, as an interest in increasing desirable characteristics within a population. But in practice eugenics quickly evolved into an obsession with identifying, quantifying, and eliminating "undesirable" characteristics... as well as the people thought to possess them. The popularity of eugenics in American culture and its influence on the US government remain a dark part of United States history that few like to acknowledge.

As far as we know, the concept of eugenics began with Plato's *Republic* in the fourth century BCE. In Book III, Plato has his protagonist, Socrates, argue that the best way to make sure the right people rule in an ideal city-state is to tell the people a story that makes their suitability for ruling self-evident. Tell them, he said, that as creatures of the earth, every person is born with a certain precious metal in their soul. Those with gold belong to the guardian class, from which the leaders should always be selected.

The auxiliary class, who are the soldiers and defenders, have silver. And the producer class, who are the farmers and laborers, have bronze. The city can never be ruled by someone with the wrong metals mixed in their blood, Plato has Socrates explain, or else it will be destroyed.

To prevent that from ever happening, Plato suggested the creation of a state-run mating program that matched highly desirable men and women, while controlling or precluding matches with and between the lower classes. The program would use a secretly rigged lottery. A lottery, presumably to make its participants feel like they had a shot at some good luck and weren't just hamsters on someone else's wheel. Rigged, to make sure the right hamsters found the right luck on the proper wheels. And secret, because even back then someone as wise as Plato knew an idea like this would *not* go over well. In a stratified society like ancient Greece, the majority of the population was never far from a reminder of their lesser status, and this plan—which has all the ingredients of a conspiracy, incidentally— was just one more for the list.

The purpose of the plan is clear: strengthen (or purify) the guardian class. Make sure the wisest, most virtuous members of society produced nothing but wiser and more virtuous offspring, who would then lead the state in the next generation. If the state could pair off the golden souled through this fixed lottery, then they could control and direct the growth of the population toward a more perfect city-state. To its *Platonic* ideal, you could say.

The *Republic* has stood as a foundational work of moral and political philosophy in the Western canon for more than 2,000 years, but these little conspiratorial seeds of social engineering managed to slip quietly through the cracks for most of that time. It wasn't until the end of the nineteenth century, in England, that they sprouted up and were nurtured into what is our modern understanding of eugenics by a natural scientist named Francis Galton.

Francis Galton was obsessed with two things: improving humanity and quantifying everything in his presence. In his twenties and thirties, on a grand tour of the African continent, Galton took latitude, longitude, and altitude measurements everywhere he went. When he wasn't measuring the geography, he was trying to measure the people. Specifically, the butt sizes of the various tribespeople he encountered on his travels. (No, that isn't a joke.) Back in Britain, he developed a method for cataloging fingerprints that Scotland Yard eventually adopted into their investigative procedures. He published an empirical analysis of the efficacy of prayer. He was the first man to ever create a weather map. And he even had the audacity to develop a beauty map, ranking the relative attractiveness of the women from every corner of the British Isles.

But it was the work of Galton's cousin, Charles Darwin, and the publication of *On the Origin of Species* in 1859, that brought his two obsessions together. Galton was enamored of Darwin's observations about natural selection, which became the foundation of evolutionary theory. Darwin's illustrative use of artificial selection in agriculture and animal husbandry to explain how evolutionary selection pressures work in nature ignited within Galton a passion for using science to improve the human race. He took the concept of "survival of the fittest" and asked: How does it work in human populations, and can it be used to make society better?

Galton didn't wait around for someone else to give him the answers. He got to work studying the pedigrees of notable British families and, in 1865, published a paper called "Hereditary Talent and Character" in one of the most popular and respected British magazines of the Victorian age. His hypothesis was that talent and character were heritable traits and that, if he was right, society's most prominent and successful men would have sons who boasted similar credentials.[4] That was precisely what he found. His findings then motivated him to expand and deepen his research, analyzing the pedigrees of prominent men from all across society and even digging into obituaries in an effort to make his study multigenerational. In the end, he calculated that intelligence and a multitude of other desirable skills were also significantly heritable. This time, Galton published his

---

[4] Galton focused on fathers and sons not because he believed talent and character were heritable on the Y chromosome; this was simply the byproduct of studying "success" in a chauvinistic patriarchal society.

findings in a book called *Hereditary Genius*. Heredity, he asserted, was the primary driver of talent, character, and, therefore, success in the human species. And if we'd just let natural selection do its thing instead of getting in the way of it like humans have a tendency to do,[5] the human race would be leaps and bounds ahead of where it found itself. Galton's suggestion was for an institutionalized practice of arranged marriages between high-status people that would select for all these desirable, heritable traits and ultimately produce better humans. A superior race. A more perfect world.

This was the first articulation of a theory of eugenics and a first glimpse at what a eugenics policy might look like. Sounds downright Platonic, doesn't it? A little Ku Klux Klan-y, perhaps?

Obviously, there are big holes in Galton's methodology and assumptions. Today they would not be considered particularly scientific. For example, there was no attempt to control for the impact of environmental benefits like privilege and patronage and education—everything that comprises the "nurture" side of the nature versus nurture debate, basically. But none of that slowed the adoption of Galton's conclusions by the very segment of society he had studied. Even his cousin was on board. In a letter sent shortly after the publication of Galton's book, Darwin wrote to him: "I do not think I ever in all of my life have read anything more interesting and original."[6] In *The Descent of Man*, Darwin's 1871 follow-up treatise on sexual selection, he engaged earnestly and repeatedly with many of Galton's eugenic ideas, as if they represented a final scientific consensus on the subject of heredity and human advancement.

Debate over the scope and pace of human evolution continued long past Darwin's death in 1882. But very little of it, regardless of which direction the evolutionary wind blew, affected the trajectory of what was becoming

---

[5] When Galton discovered that the lower classes of society were having more babies and growing faster than Britain's "guardian class," he didn't think he needed to reevaluate his methodology or his hypothesis. Instead, he urgently argued for ways to make sure rich people had kids with other rich people and for poor people to have fewer kids or, preferably, no kids at all.

[6] This comes from a letter Darwin wrote to Galton on December 23, 1859, which appears as LETTER 410 in *The Letters of Charles Darwin*.

a eugenics *movement*. The popularity of eugenic ideas was helped by the Industrial Revolution, which was bringing more and more workers from rural towns and villages into contact with immigrant and minority populations in cities like London, Boston, and New York, where all the jobs were increasingly concentrated. The predominantly white Anglo-European majority began to perceive these "strangers" (as they were sometimes euphemistically described) as threats to their prospects for wealth and status. Not just that, they laid everything that was going wrong with society in the turbulent decades around the turn of the twentieth century at the feet of these "other" people as well. To improve society and to protect their place in it, those who felt most threatened believed something had to be done. For many, this new concept of eugenics, if embedded into new laws, looked like it could be that something. Something that promised to boost the signal of all the good heritable traits (according to them) and drown out the noise coming from all the weak, destructive traits—producing an improved human race and a better, more stable world (for them) as a result.

With that worldview and its reliance on still poorly understood science as the foundation for public policy, it is a minor miracle that no eugenics laws were ever passed in Britain during this period. The United States, on the other hand, well, that's a different bag of unnaturally selected badgers.

THE POSITIVE AND NEGATIVE OF A MORE "PERFECT" UNION

AMERICAN SCIENTISTS AND POLITICIANS flirted with eugenics policies as early as the late 1890s. Connecticut and Michigan, for example, tried passing eugenics-inspired laws in 1896 and 1897. But it wasn't until Gregor

40

Mendel's work with pea plants and heredity was rediscovered by the first generation of geneticists in 1900 that things really started to take off.

One of the scientists to embrace Mendel's work was an American biologist and chicken breeder named Charles Davenport. In Mendelian principles, with their recognition of dominant and recessive inheritance, Davenport saw the scientific mechanism behind what animal breeders had been doing with livestock for centuries: selectively breeding their animals for specific, desirable traits. Davenport was also a fan of Francis Galton's work and had studied large families much the way Galton had, for much the same reason. He was excited at the prospect of combining all these influences in the study of people—applying Mendelian rules of inheritance to the selection of specific, desirable traits in an effort to improve the human race. So in 1910, Davenport created something called the Eugenics Record Office (ERO) out of a laboratory on Long Island, New York. For the next thirty years, researchers at the ERO collated and analyzed biographical information from hundreds of thousands of people with the stated intent to "improve the natural, physical, mental, and temperamental qualities of the human family."[7]

This is where things start to break bad with eugenics and where minority populations really start to find themselves in the crosshairs of state and national governments. Because there are two kinds of eugenics: positive and negative.[8] The positive kind is idealistic. It's what Plato and Galton and Davenport spent most of their time talking about, at least at first. Selecting for the best traits. Encouraging people with those traits to marry and procreate. Rigging the system for that to happen, if necessary. Then sitting back and watching as Utopia slowly unfolded in front of them.

Positive eugenics, in that sense, was about building a better mousetrap.

Except, for a confirmed eugenicist, you can't have the positive without dealing with the negative, as Galton found out when he realized that the "weaker" lower classes of British society were procreating more successfully

---

[7] From an ERO publication released circa 1927.

[8] We don't mean this figuratively; this is literally what they are called by social scientists—positive eugenics and negative eugenics.

than the "stronger" upper classes. It doesn't matter whether talent and character are heritable traits among folks of noble bearing if they're having fewer offspring than those deemed to be of lesser stock. On that trend line, the "meek" *will* inherit the earth eventually. It also doesn't matter from a Mendelian perspective if "good" traits are dominant or "bad" traits are recessive. If two recessive carriers produce offspring, it will be recessive, just as two dominant carriers will produce a dominant offspring.[9]

Which brings us back to the basic math of procreation and forward to the rise of negative eugenics. If the game is simply a matter of who produces more progeny by the time the clock runs out, the easiest way to make sure the "good" guys always win is to prohibit as many "bad" guys as possible from getting a chance to play. That is the thrust of negative eugenics. It's deeply cynical. It's about making the mousetrap foolproof by keeping the mouse out of the house altogether.

To your run-of-the-mill early-1900s eugenicist, one can imagine the practical appeal of negative eugenics. After all, it's much easier to prevent something from happening than it is to make something happen. Prohibiting behavior is far simpler than promoting it. That's why every eugenics organization and legislative initiative between 1900 and 1940 turned away from positive eugenics as a way to "improve . . . the human family" and focused instead on eliminating undesirable traits. In pouring over reams of generational family data, as well as the biographical information of inmates in the country's prisons and psychiatric hospitals (they called them "asylums" back then), scientists at institutions like the ERO and the Race Betterment Foundation sought to establish the genetic heritability of bad traits and then use their findings to promote policies that would prohibit individuals who possessed those traits from having kids and

---

9   Ironically, for eugenicists who hadn't fully grasped Mendelian genetics, appearing to be a dominant carrier does not guarantee a dominant offspring. If both parents are phenotypically dominant (that is, they physically express the dominant trait) but are actually genotypic hybrids (that is, they carry the dominant and the recessive trait), they have a one-in-four chance of producing a recessive offspring.

perpetuating the traits into the future. "Unfit" is how those individuals were categorized.

If that sounds like a scientific rationale for cleansing, that's because it is.

It should surprise no one then—least of all those who have felt targeted for exclusion by society in the past—that the people found to be unfit by eugenicists belonged overwhelmingly to poor, minority, and immigrant populations. It should be equally unsurprising that, among the Anglo-European majority, eugenicists found widespread support for their conclusions and many of their subsequent policy recommendations: marriage restrictions, immigration restrictions, indefinite institutionalization, forced sterilization, and, to a lesser extent, euthanasia.

That's right. *Euthanasia.*

By the 1930s, a number of medical organizations and prominent physicians had been openly advocating for and abiding the killing of the unfit for years. In two separate instances in the winter of 1915, for instance, a doctor in Chicago named Harry Haiselden refused to perform necessary surgery on newborn infants with severe birth defects and allowed them to die. He would condemn as many as four other babies to the same fate over the next few years, going so far as to display the infants to journalists and to write about his work for the Hearst newspaper empire. In 1935, a British doctor similarly admitted to killing five incurable patients, including a baby who he determined was "doomed to imbecility." These physicians had no shortage of detractors in the medical community, to be sure, but they also had more than their fair share of support from notable figures like Clarence Darrow and Helen Keller, and organizations like the Illinois Homeopathic Medical Association and the Euthanasia Society of America, who were just as concerned with "killing defectives on eugenic grounds" as they were with what was supposedly their primary mission—alleviating the suffering of the terminally ill.[10] "What is the use in saving them?" the famed pathologist

---

[10] "Defective" wasn't even the worst thing the "unfit" were called, whether they were babies or the adults who conceived them. They were called "imbeciles," "feebleminded," and "human mental monstrosities."

Aldred Scott Warthin asked in 1930. "There are too many people living now without whom the world would be much better off!"[11]

Interestingly, public support for euthanasia was not so broad or openly callous. Nor was it consistently applied to everyone. In 1937, a popular magazine conducted a poll about euthanasia and found that among those who didn't completely oppose it, far more people were in favor of terminating "defective" babies than helping the incurably sick. The difference in opinion, it appears, was due at least in part to the perceived eugenic benefit of nipping unfitness in the bud. If there was an upside to the general discomfort with euthanasia for eugenicists, it was that it made less severe policies—in particular, forced sterilization—seem humane, if not downright charitable. Something their advocates took great advantage of.

> **There are too many people living now without whom the world would be much better off!**
>
> **— ALDRED SCOTT WARTHIN**

Between 1900 and 1940, thirty-two states passed sterilization laws aimed at stemming the tide of imbecility, epilepsy, criminality, insanity, feeblemindedness, and other vaguely defined conditions with supposedly strong genetic components found mostly in poor, minority, and immigrant populations. In the middle of that period, Congress passed the Immigration Act of 1924, which curtailed immigration from the predominantly Catholic and the not coincidentally more darkly complected regions of southern and eastern Europe, while virtually eliminating immigration from Asia entirely. In 1927, by a vote of eight to one, the United States Supreme Court upheld a state's right to sterilize a person who it considered unfit to procreate—in this case, a Virginia woman named Carrie Buck. She'd been institutionalized by her foster parents for moral delinquency (specifically, having children out of wedlock), deemed feebleminded by the state's doctors, and

---

[11] Warthin's primary work was on the heritability of cancer. He would ultimately be remembered as the father of cancer genetics.

then sterilized under the Virginia Eugenical Sterilization Act, which had been passed the very same year as Congress passed the Immigration Act.

Inspired by these laws, in 1933 the Nazi Party in Germany instituted its own "sterilization and purification" program, which culminated a decade later with the systematic murder of 6 million Jews, as well as other "undesirables," including gay men, the disabled, and the Roma. By the time the horrors of the Holocaust were revealed to the world at the end of World War II in 1945, tens of thousands of Americans had been sterilized under government orders in the United States.[12] By the end of the twentieth century, that number would climb to approximately 70,000, including 25 percent of all Native American women of childbearing age, many of whom underwent sterilization without their consent during other surgical procedures or as part of a devil's bargain in exchange for health-care services for their children. Seventy thousand human beings! That's the size of the entire Black population of central Harlem in 1991, where the fifty-cent soda flyers saw some of their widest distribution.

Is it any wonder that there are persistent fears of sterilization within the Black community, within poor neighborhoods, within groups disproportionately represented in criminal and mental institutions, where the bulk of forced sterilizations took place in those years? Just think about this from the perspective of the Black experience in America for one second. The story begins with 250 years of chattel slavery, during which time slaves were often compelled by their masters to breed, like livestock, in order to produce babies who would then become the property of the slaveowners. This was followed by four years of horrifically bloody civil war between 1861 and 1865 that led to the passage of the Thirteenth Amendment and the abolition of slavery, only to be countered almost immediately with Black codes and Jim Crow laws designed to control where newly "free" Black

---

[12] Adolf Hitler was a great admirer of American eugenicists and followed the movement closely as he rose to power. "I have studied with interest the laws of several American states concerning prevention of reproduction by people whose progeny would, in all probability, be of no value or be injurious to the racial stock," he told Otto Wagener, head of the Nazi Party's Economic Policy Office.

45

people could live, work, eat, sleep, drink, breathe, pray, sing, go to the bathroom, you name it. And when that wasn't good enough, scientists, doctors, educators, and politicians figured out a way to use two brand-new scientific discoveries—evolution and genetics—as the justification for wiping Blacks off the face of the map entirely. For the good of the "human family."

One lesson from this story is that if the government couldn't control you, they would conspire to eliminate you. And if they couldn't do that, well, then they might just use you like a lab rat, and not tell you, like they did with more than 600 Black men beginning right around the peak of the eugenics movement in 1932.

THE TRAGEDY OF TUSKEGEE

AS EUGENICS THEORY MADE ITS WAY deeper into state houses and hospitals and laboratories around the country, the US government launched one of the most infamous conspiracies against its people in American history. In 1932, in a small city called Tuskegee tucked into the eastern edge of Alabama, researchers from the US Public Health Service (PHS) and the Tuskegee Normal and Industrial Institute (what is today Tuskegee University) joined forces to enlist several hundred poor, local Black sharecroppers for a syphilis study.

At the time there was no clear treatment for syphilis. Today, we understand it is a bacterial infection primarily contracted through sexual intercourse. But back then, syphilis was considered more than a medical problem. It was also viewed as a consequence of immoral behavior—the kind that got people like Carrie Buck and her mother, Emma, institutionalized and, ultimately, in Carrie's case at least, involuntarily sterilized.[13] Left untreated, syphilis can lead to a number of chronic, painful conditions—anything from blindness to bone deterioration. In extreme cases, it can cause death. Today it is a curable condition when caught early enough and treated with a single shot of penicillin. Yet in the 1930s the "great pox" was considered both powerful and deadly, having spread deep into the population—especially in the impoverished rural South.

The tragedy of Tuskegee begins when the eggheads at the PHS find themselves at a crossroads at some point in 1931 or 1932. For a few years prior, the PHS had been working with a Chicago-based charity called the Julius Rosenwald Fund[14] to test and treat for syphilis throughout the Deep South. The collaboration began in 1928, after the PHS had completed a study of the more than 2,000 Black employees at a massive Mississippi cotton plantation. The Rosenwald Fund, looking to extend the reach of their philanthropic work, committed to paying for the treatment of those who tested positive for syphilis (approximately a quarter of the workforce). On the back of that successful effort, they then launched a joint five-county pilot program aimed at demonstrating the feasibility of testing and treating "rural blacks" in a similar fashion, but on a larger scale. For the next three years, from 1929 to 1931, the Rosenwald Fund bankrolled the testing efforts of PHS staff in Albemarle County, Virginia; Glynn County, Georgia; Pitt County, North Carolina; Tipton County, Tennessee; and Macon County, Alabama—of which Tuskegee is the seat.[15]

As the treatment phase of the program was set to begin, however, the money ran out. The stock market crash of 1929, and the economic collapse that followed, had finally taken its toll on the coffers of the Rosenwald Fund.

---

[13] Emma Buck had been institutionalized for moral delinquency and feeblemindedness because she was found guilty of prostitution and having syphilis.

[14] Julius Rosenwald was one of the co-owners of Sears, Roebuck and Co. and a major philanthropist in the areas of equal opportunity, education, and health, especially as it related to rural southern Blacks.

[15] If you were committed to beating back a raging inferno of something like syphilis, there were few better places to dig your firebreaks than these five counties.

Its administrators realized they could no longer fund the program. The question then became: What was the PHS going to do? Because their interest in continuing their syphilis work was still very much alive. In their estimation, they'd made a real difference down in places like Macon County. They'd earned the trust and cooperation of state health officials as well as community leaders and educators at places like the Tuskegee Institute. There was a legitimately productive working relationship in place that the PHS didn't just want to give up on. They wanted to make something out of all this work. They just had to figure out what they could do when they no longer had the money to do anything.

THE ORIGINS OF SYPHILIS

Much of the modern narrative around Christopher Columbus centers on the diseases that he and his crew brought with them on their voyages to the New World in the 1490s. Old, familiar afflictions like typhoid, measles, smallpox, and flu burned through the virgin soil of what is today called the Bahamas and decimated native populations over the ensuing years.

The exchange was not one-sided, however. Historians and epidemiological researchers believe that Columbus's crew brought syphilis back to the Old World from Hispaniola. The debate is not fully settled, and it appears that variants of the bacterium that causes syphilis have been bouncing around potentially for millennia, but it seems fairly certain that the version of the highly contagious venereal syphilis that we encounter today—and that was the subject of the Tuskegee syphilis experiment—has its origins in the New World. It arrived on European shores in 1493, tore through a garrison of French soldiers fighting in Naples, Italy, in 1495, and from there spread across the world as the age of exploration connected the globe.[16]

---

[16] Syphilis actually gets its name from a sixteenth-century Latin epic poem published by Girolamo Fracastoro, whose title translates to "Syphilis, or the French Disease."

They found their solution in a 1928 study out of Norway that had turned the assumptions of the American scientific establishment on their heads. In line with much of the thinking around race that emerged from the eugenics movement, American scientists had long believed that syphilis affected white patients and Black patients differently. White people suffered primarily neurological symptoms, they asserted, while Black patients suffered predominantly cardiovascular problems. What Norwegian researchers found from their study of a group made up entirely of white men in Oslo was a preponderance of cardiovascular issues and no meaningful presence of neurological deficit. Essentially, the American understanding of syphilis was completely wrong (and totally racist).

Researchers at the PHS became convinced that they needed to more clearly and completely understand the disease, and to do that they needed to conduct a *prospective* study where they closely observed the effects syphilis had on the human body when left to develop unchecked.[17] That's how they would rescue what might have otherwise felt like three years of wasted testing in those five rural counties: they would design a study that not only didn't require any substantive treatment but specifically precluded it!

When it came to putting the study together, there was no easy solution. Advertising a paid study in the local newspapers wasn't likely to get the candidates they needed, as the only people willing to go on record with the condition were likely already too far along to be of much use. People who realized they had contracted syphilis, though still in the early stages, were also not likely to out themselves, regardless of whatever anonymity might be offered. In the teeth of the Great Depression, when work was scarce but workers were not, you didn't intentionally make life more complicated for yourself unless you had absolutely no other choice.

---

[17] In contrast, the Norwegian study was retrospective. It enrolled people with the disease and looked backward, using personal, biographical data collected from the participants to make determinations related to causality, risk, and other related factors. This was effectively the same methodology that Francis Galton used in "Hereditary Talent and Character" and Charles Davenport used at the ERO.

And so the US Public Health Service committed one of the great ethical crimes of the era. To make it all happen, they purposely sought out the most vulnerable and lied to them, exploiting the goodwill and long-standing relationship they'd built with administrators and faculty at the Tuskegee Institute in the process. The choice of Macon County as the site for the study, and Tuskegee in particular as its center, was a natural fit for the PHS. Nearly 40 percent of the tested population in Macon had syphilis, so the pool of candidates was large. Tuskegee was also the headquarters of National Negro Health Week, which had been started in 1915 by the school's first president, Booker T. Washington, and had then been taken over by the PHS in 1930 in an effort to make it a national movement. National Negro Health Week was the perfect time to recruit subjects for the study and to conduct subsequent annual exams, which were part of the study's design. With the help of researchers at the institute, the PHS began posting flyers that offered to treat "bad blood" in exchange for free medical care, free meals after examinations, and fifty-dollar burial insurance to anyone who signed an autopsy consent form.[18]

You might be saying to yourself: *Autopsy consent form? That's morbid.* It is, and it speaks to the true intentions of the syphilis study. At no point did the PHS have plans to help the men with the thing they were actually trying to study. They just wanted to see what happened, to learn how syphilis worked. They called it studying "the natural history" of the disease. Much like the science—and the scientists—behind eugenics, the rationalizations for this apparent lack of humanity were rooted in the prevalent classism and racism of the time. It wasn't as if these guys would have received any medical care to begin with, they told themselves. These folks would be over the moon just for the exam and the meal and the comfort that came with knowing their families wouldn't have to worry about paying for their funerals.

---

[18] "Bad blood" was a regional umbrella term from the period used to describe everything from anemia to fatigue to tuberculosis, as well as syphilis.

A COMPLICATED LEGACY

Booker T. Washington is a seminal figure in the fight for equality in America. A brilliant educator and activist, Washington fought for advancements in health, education, and business for Black people across the country, but particularly in the South. This work brought him inside powerful circles, including the administrations of multiple US presidents. It also brought him into contact with a number of people whose fingerprints are all over the eugenics movement and the Tuskegee study.

In 1912, Washington invited Julius Rosenwald to sit on the board of the Tuskegee Institute, which invariably smoothed the way for the PHS to come in and do much of their work in Macon County. In 1913, he wrote to Charles Davenport and invited him to visit the school. Davenport wouldn't make it down before Washington's death in 1915, but the entreaty would lead to an entirely different study commissioned by the Eugenics Record Office in 1932 that involved taking 131 "anthropometric measurements" of 200 Black students in Tuskegee and following them like a school class for the next dozen years as part of their "scientific" effort "to define Negro race."

As an astute political operator and as the leader of the southern Black elite at the turn of the twentieth century, Washington was of the mind that the best way to effect change was from within, by Black people lifting themselves up and simultaneously using the tools of the establishment against itself. His invitation to Rosenwald, for example, brought a big-city business magnate inside the walls of the Tuskegee Institute, which was, at the time, essentially a vocational school. His letter to Davenport was an attempt to open the door for eugenicists to use their methods to collect data that would disprove their own theses.

Beyond being somewhat naive with respect to how much a well-meaning rich white person might actually do for the cause of equality, or with respect to the rigor and objectivity of the ideas coming out of places like the ERO, Washington put himself in a position to be criticized and labeled as accommodationist by some of his contemporaries, particularly those in the North, such as W. E. B. DuBois.

With time, Washington's legacy has found its fullest and fairest interpretation. He will rightly remain a revered icon in the history of the ongoing struggle for equality and the advancement of Black people in the United States.

And the PHS apologists were right. To many of the desperately poor farmers who enrolled in the study, the offer was too good to pass up. "We could not get health care. We were poor. We could not get anybody in the city to help us in the country," said Herman Shaw, one of the subjects who survived long enough to attend the official, ceremonial government apology for the study at the White House in 1997. It was a godsend, he told the *Baltimore Sun* at the age of ninety-five, while recognizing at the same time that "really...we were forced into it" by circumstance.

All in all, the PHS enrolled 600 men from Macon County in this study. Three hundred ninety-nine had latent syphilis, while 201 others who were infection-free were used as a control group. The men swindled into this study were no less intelligent than the Norwegians cited in the 1928 study, nor were they any less intelligent than the average American. It is highly likely that if they had been given more information about the true purpose of the initiative, they would have refused to participate.

And so the PHS never mentioned the "S-word." They also never mentioned that the treatments they were providing weren't treatments at all. While the men were under the impression they were being given free medical care for "bad blood," the PHS gave the entirety of the group placebos such as aspirin or innocuous mineral supplements.

Their goal was never to "cure" syphilis, nor was it to assist these men with the various medical conditions they may have been suffering from. Instead, Uncle Sam wanted them on the hook, as canaries in an STD coal mine. They fed them fake drugs and carefully monitored how the symptoms of syphilis advanced inexorably from one stage to the next. This would go on for *forty years*, resulting in the deaths of at least 128 of the participants. Many of them would die without knowing the real name of the project they had effectively signed their lives away to: "The Tuskegee Study of Untreated Syphilis in the Negro Male."

The Tuskegee study took on an insidious institutional life all its own. One that only ended in 1972 because a whistleblower inside the PHS leaked the details of the study and the story ended up on the front page of the *New York Times*. To put this four-decade-long conspiracy into perspective, the initiative continued through multiple presidential administrations under both political parties and under the leadership of multiple government officials. Over the decades, the PHS, like almost any nonmilitary government agency, battled budget cuts—and they always chose to continue their grotesque activities in Alabama, sending new junior researchers down to Macon County every year to conduct the annual exams and, one suspects, avoid the accumulation of too much institutional memory, lest someone be overcome by a fit of conscience. The government learned penicillin could be an effective treatment for syphilis in 1947, fifteen years after the study began. The PHS did . . . nothing. PHS staffers and local doctors complicit in the conspiracy watched as innocent men lost their eyesight, lost their minds, and lost their lives.

The story of Tuskegee is, at heart, the story of three great injustices. First and foremost, it is a study of immorality. The PHS could have, at any point, attempted to treat its victims. Post-1947, the PHS could have easily administered penicillin. It did not. Secondly, and again at any point, the PHS could have told these men the true aim of its

The story of Tuskegee is, at heart, the story of three great injustices.

initiative. It did not. Third, and perhaps most damning, at least some part of the modern Western world's inherent distrust of medicine arrives directly from this indisputable fact: the US government conspired to watch these people die, all the while assuring them a cure was just around the corner, just to see what would happen.

The Tuskegee syphilis experiment and the eugenics movement that preceded it (if not outright ushered it into being) are arguably part of the reason so many Americans are quick to believe that the government is up to some terrible mad science in hidden laboratories across the continent, even today. This is especially true for Black Americans, many of whom were raised hearing stories from the eugenics movement and from Tuskegee about relatives and family friends who weren't just part of these terrible experiments—*they were the experiments*. When you hear stories like these, stories about sinister experiments on innocent people, it can be difficult not to wonder: "Well, what else?"

MK ULTRA: A DEATH COUNT OF ONE . . . OFFICIALLY

Sometime around two am on November 28, 1953, a government scientist from Fort Detrick, Maryland named Frank Olson falls to his death from a room at the Statler Hotel in New York City. The government tells Olson's family that he died in the course of his work. An internal investigation by the CIA in the weeks after Olson's death concludes that he'd jumped as a "result of circumstances arising out of [an] experiment" conducted by the agency a week earlier at a retreat on Deep Creek Lake in Maryland. They'd dosed Olson and some of his fellow scientists with LSD supposedly to test their trustworthiness and their susceptibility to suggestion. Why? Olson and company worked in the biowarfare laboratories at Fort Detrick, which was home not just to the country's bioweapons program but also to a new, highly sensitive experimental mind control program called MK Ultra, which principally used LSD in an effort to control and manipulate human consciousness (i.e., brainwash). The program had been approved by CIA Director Allen Dulles barely six months earlier. It would last another twenty years in almost total secrecy and include nearly 150 human experiments, two dozen of which involved unwitting participants . . . including Frank Olson. His would be the only officially reported death in connection with the program.

And when that question starts to float around in your head, it's hard not to find proof of what you're looking for. (Confirmation bias strikes again!) That's precisely how these sterilization conspiracies have proliferated. Whether it's the Church's Chicken conspiracy in the mid-1980s, the fifty-cent soda conspiracy in 1991, or more recently, COVID-19 vaccination hesitancy. When the pop star Nicki Minaj tweeted in September 2021 that she wasn't vaccinated because her cousin's friend down in the Dominican Republic had been vaccinated and suffered horrible side effects that ultimately cost him his relationship with his fiancée, it was no coincidence that the one side effect she mentioned was impotence.

It makes sense when you take a look at the parallels. The COVID vaccine is a new medicine being offered for free by the government to treat a brutal infection that is disproportionately affecting poor, minority, and immigrant communities. Where have we seen this movie before? Oh, that's right: *history*.

THE RHYME OF HISTORY

FOR THOSE IN THE BUSINESS OF BATTLING BACK against a rising tide of misinformation and conspiracy theories, it is tempting to look at events like the eugenics movement and the Tuskegee experiment as singular moments in time. They are products of exceptional circumstances, well-meaning but misguided figures, wrong turns accidentally made at pivotal crossroads. That is often the kind of explanation you will hear from someone who doesn't want to reckon with the reality of government power.

Here is the truth: history overflows with examples of the powerful experimenting on the powerless without their consent. Human experiments predate the earliest days of modern science, as well as the term "experiment" itself. It is genuinely difficult to find any period of human history wherein people *weren't* conducting unethical, unclean experiments on one another.

Just consider the ancient conceit of a "natural language." The idea was that if a child survived birth and grew up with minimal human interaction, it would speak the secret language of the gods. As far back as the fifth century BCE, we find accounts of societies experimenting on children in an effort to understand this language, and language in general. In his *Histories*, the ancient Greek historian Herodotus writes about an Egyptian pharaoh named Psamtik.[19] This pharaoh is a real pill; he isolates newborns in an attempt to understand how human language develops. Spoiler alert: those children die. Nearly 2,000 years later, in the thirteenth century CE, the Holy Roman emperor Frederick II raises children with minimal social interaction to see whether they eventually speak a common, "natural" tongue. (They do not.) Toward the close of the fifteenth century, historians argue James IV of Scotland, curious about the origin of language itself, sends two toddlers off to live with a mute woman on an island at the mouth of the North Sea. The medieval monarchs all want to know: Does language spring forth naturally, or is it learned?

Those are three shockingly similar experiments. Each separated by hundreds of years and thousands of miles. Each involving a society's most vulnerable and voiceless populations, perpetrated by that society's most powerful figures.

Obviously, this pattern is not unique to the subject of language or human communication. It emerges whenever society faces difficult, pressing questions that the government has a strong, vested interest in discovering the answers to. The stronger the interest, and the more pressing or difficult the

---

[19] Psamtik—also known as Psammetichus I—ruled from 664 to 610 BCE, during the Twenty-Sixth Dynasty of Egypt. He died more than 200 years before Herodotus penned his Histories. Like many writers of his age, Herodotus was doing his best with limited resources—back in his day, rumors and conjecture were often treated as fact. The rise of social media has arguably created a similar situation here in the twenty-first century.

question (in the eyes of the government at least), the more likely a government is to treat its people as disposable or fungible in pursuit of the answer, even if that is not expressly its intention.

That's how we ended up where we did in the first quarter of the twentieth century with the sterilization campaigns, immigration restrictions, and marriage laws that defined the eugenics movement. Industrialization and mass immigration were changing the complexion of the country in a way that felt like an existential threat to those in power, and so the society's institutions jumped into action with little regard for the humanity of those who were associated with "the problem."

In the 1930s and 1940s, the Black farmers in the Tuskegee experiment were considered expendable because syphilis had become a scourge of epidemic proportions. It was a public health emergency, talked about much the way AIDS would be talked about in the 1980s and '90s. If it took 600 poor, unwitting rural farmers to fully understand this brutal disease, and that understanding then led to a cure or to better strategies for preventing the disease's spread, then how could you not excuse what the PHS did?

That was the exact rationale of the US Court of Appeals, incidentally, in its 1983 decision to dismiss the case brought against the federal government by the family of Edward Nevin in the aftermath of Operation Moby Dick. The government had good intentions, the court held. It was trying to protect the country from the threat of biological attack. If it were liable anytime it made an honest mistake, the government wouldn't be able to fulfill its duty. Essentially, if you want to make an omelet, you've got to crack some eggs. The fact that those eggs, if left undisturbed, would grow into chickens, doesn't make the chef liable for murder.

That is the argument. What it fails to consider is that by allowing government agencies and established institutions to use people as test subjects without their consent, all in the name of the greater good, what you are doing is sowing seeds of distrust. These seeds inevitably grow into the kinds of conspiracy theories that get in the way of legitimate good works when they are most critical.

CHAPTER THREE
SURVEILLANCE

FOR DECADES, IT WAS AN OLD CLICHÉ: "YOU HAVE TO BE CAREFUL," says the paranoid, tinfoil-hat-wearing wingnut. "They're watching us." For decades, whenever some allegation about ever-present snooping sounded a little too out-there, a little too conspiratorial, authorities and pundits on the news were quick to dismiss it as the ramblings of an unbalanced mind. These days, one of the most prevalent examples of this sort of paranoia can be found in gang-stalking conspiracy theories, the idea that unnamed groups of individuals are surreptitiously monitoring someone for nefarious, often unnamed purposes.

One of the most recent, admittedly far-out conspiracy theories in the realm of surveillance concerns the administration of the COVID-19 vaccines. Back in 2020, a Facebook video went viral, claiming that every vaccine would contain a radio frequency identification (or RFID) microchip capable of tracking, in great detail, the activities of vaccinated individuals. The video was shared widely across the social media platform, sparking alarm as viewers who were already deeply distrustful of the government swallowed the story hook, line, and sinker. There's just one problem: it was utterly, purposely false. The video itself is pretty short—at just under four minutes, it's an amalgamation of out-of-context interviews and statements, carefully curated so as to beguile unwitting audience members into believing a shadowy cabal of the rich and powerful have either planned the pandemic or used it as an opportunity to institute an unprecedented global surveillance system.

The video itself is easily debunked. It builds off statements from people like Jay Walker, executive chairman of a company called ApiJect, which manufactures, among other things, prefilled syringes. In a May 2020 interview, Walker talked about the option of using an RFID chip as a part of the label attached to a syringe. The chips, he points out, wouldn't contain personal information since they would be included in the initial manufacturing process, and their sole purpose would be to help medical staff to confirm the vaccine within was both unexpired and authentic. This story was distorted to give rise to a conspiracy. It's just one part of a massive propaganda campaign to cast aspersion on vaccination and, often, the idea of COVID-19 in general, even as millions died from the infection and related complications.

Bill Gates features heavily in this and other videos. It's fair to say the billionaire, philanthropist, and founder of Microsoft is the unwitting star of these and other related conspiracies. His advocacy for vaccination has made him a target of the antivaccine movement for years, well before the rise of COVID-19. Additionally, Gates warned about the possibility of a new pandemic as far back as 2015. We predicted something similar on our show—this wasn't an act of precognition, just an objective assessment of global trends.

For those who already distrust the wealthy (with good reason) and who fear government medical malpractice due to historic crimes like the Tuskegee experiments, it doesn't seem too far a leap to go from the idea that Gates was warning about an outbreak to claiming that he, in fact, for some reason, helped orchestrate it. The truth is much less interesting: Gates has never proposed that vaccines include a means of actively tracking or "controlling" people.

His primary philanthropic organization, the Bill and Melinda Gates Foundation, did fund a pilot study looking into the possibility of a vaccine-delivery mechanism that could leave an invisible mark detectable by a smartphone. This study, published in *Science Translational Medicine* in December 2019, does read a bit like science fiction, and it should. All accounts of the actual study confirm it was theoretical, and if it ever did make it off the figurative drawing board, it would function as a passive form of confirmation, as opposed to an active form of tracking activity.

This isn't to say Gates *doesn't* want to track people in one way or another—the COVID-19 conspiracy takes another bad-faith boost from an additional public health idea championed by Gates: the "digital identity." Put simply, a digital identity would be a kind of personal record system in the cloud—accessible only with the owner's consent but available anywhere in the world. This could be tremendously useful in situations where, say, a person vacationing abroad needs medical attention, or a surgeon working remotely needs access to a patient's records in preparation for a procedure.

The most prominent source of funding for this research comes from a nonprofit called the Digital Identity Alliance, popularly known as ID2020. This concept of digital identity does not require a microchip or other invasive surgery, but for true believers it functions as a kind of foreshadowing. In the minds of those who believe this conspiracy, Gates's support of the digital identity speaks to his motivation to further control the world's population. (To what end, no one knows.) The conspiracy theory also touches on the idea of contact tracing, which countries like South Korea and Israel have used to effectively map the transmission of the virus. Contact tracing doesn't involve subcutaneous microchips, but uses the powers of government surveillance to identify how a person testing positive for COVID-19 may have acquired the infection or passed it to others. These systems use smartphone records, credit card statements, transportation records, and even CCTV footage.

The modern-day versions of our tinfoil-hatted lone wolf have genuine concerns about the world's plans to combat the virus. (In some cases, they may believe the virus itself is a hoax.) Perhaps they're sharing that viral video on various Facebook pages. Maybe they're a regular, passionate commenter on forums full of like-minded online friends. They may not be entirely clear on the endgame of this perceived conspiracy, but they're certain something's amiss, and the lack of evidence supporting this supposition is —if you think about it!— only more evidence of how pervasive and absolute the cover-up has become. And, while they're typing this on various corners of the internet, they may not know they're leaving a trail of bread crumbs, one word at a time, for a much more dangerous—and much more real—conspiracy that actively continues today.

This image of the paranoid loner, boarding up their windows, donning a cone of tinfoil, and hiding away from a supposedly vast, all-encompassing network of mass surveillance, has been around for almost a century.

This image of the paranoid loner, boarding up their windows, donning a cone of tinfoil, and hiding away from a supposedly vast, all-encompassing network of mass surveillance, has been around for almost a century. Writing for *Vice*, Roisin Kiberd traced the tinfoil hat idea back to 1927, when Julian Huxley, half brother to the novelist Aldous Huxley, penned a short story called "The Tissue-Culture King." In this story a scientist named Hascombe dabbles in mind control, eventually realizing that donning a cap made of foil will protect him against telepathy. The idea remains relevant in the modern day: it's depicted in fictional TV programs like *Better Call Saul*, in which the protagonist's elder brother, believing he suffers from electromagnetic sensitivity, eschews most modern technology and, when forced to expose himself to damaging "waves," hides beneath foil emergency blankets (the kind of thing you'd see in a survival kit). Today the stereotype is a subject of mockery, a sort of cognitive shorthand used to dismiss people as loons. While these characters are usually played for laughs in popular culture, you'd have to wonder how the so-called kooks of yesteryear would feel about the average person's online social life today.

If, for example, you're like 85 percent of Americans, you own a smartphone that you carry with you at almost all times. Through this phone, you access email, texts, and phone calls. You may have any number of apps that allow you to access your financial information, health stats, or real-world services like ordering food online or calling a car (both of which require real-time location information). Regardless of service provider or model of phone, odds are there's more information about you out there than you realize. Every click on a website, each moment spent searching or reading; these can all be scraped, collected, and analyzed to produce a stunningly accurate image of the individual using any smartphone. A growing percentage of the US population—the vast majority—has simply given over access to their personal lives.

For privacy advocates, this represents another step down a dangerous path. For some tech fans, it's just the future, as inevitable and necessary as the sunrise. For the surveillance state, it's an unprecedented leap forward, making the task of monitoring and preempting threats, avoiding other attacks like 9/11, not only much easier but morally necessary. No one in this scenario sees themselves as the "bad guy." And from the government's perspective, it's easy to understand the reasoning here: no one would want to wake up the day after a new 9/11, read the staggering death tolls, and think, *We could have stopped this, but we were concerned about privacy.*

That's the dirty, terrible thing about surveillance conspiracy theories.

YOU ARE BEING FOLLOWED

Setting aside the technical limitations and logistical infeasibility of rolling out billions of vaccine doses with individual microchips in them, there's another, much more compelling reason why the government isn't bothering to use the COVID vaccines to track people: it doesn't have to. The ordinary, on-the-grid person does the work for them, with the very objects we use to read the stories that stoke the confirmation bias we have about the government, Big Tech and Big Pharma, and our overall fears about privacy. Thanks to GPS, IP addresses, cookies, scraping algorithms, pinging cell towers, unsecured Wi-Fi hotspots, and heaven only knows what else, our smartphones, tablets, and computers let government agencies and large corporations know where we live, where we spend time, how we spend time, what we like, what we don't like, who we talk to, what we buy, what we don't buy, what we will buy, where we go, when we go, how we go. The government doesn't need a chip in a vaccine to know where you are right now. It has chips in multiple devices that we are tethered to nearly every waking hour. You are being closely followed; this is true. But it's not like that's very hard when most of us are holding devices that shout, "HEY HERE I AM!" to anyone who wants to listen.

Unlike many other tall tales of Orwellian Big Brothers, it turns out many of the accusations of massive surveillance programs are, as incredible as it might seem, absolutely true. It's often said that human civilization is in the Age of Information. The dark side of this is that we are also living in what could rightly be called the Age of Surveillance.

While the subject of mass surveillance has made headlines in recent decades, the story in the US can't be told without going back to 1791, when the Bill of Rights was passed. In it, the Fourth Amendment codified "the right of the people to be secure in their persons, houses, papers, and effects, against unreasonable searches and seizures." In practice, this meant residents of the US were protected from government snooping without probable cause, a concept that itself has been a matter of continual debate.[1] In 1928, the Supreme Court ruled that evidence from federal wiretaps was legally permissible and did not, in fact, violate the Fourth Amendment— the reasoning in this ruling, known as *Olmstead v. United States*, was that the evidence obtained in the case against a suspected bootlegger consisted of conversations over the telephone, rather than physical objects, like a letter saying, "Boy, I love bootlegging." This decision was the law of the land until it was overturned in a 1967 ruling, *Katz v. United States*.

The first law officially addressing wiretapping came about with the Federal Communications Act of 1934, which declared that wiretapping is not illegal, but information gathered via wiretap could not be publicly disclosed. For privacy advocates, this represented one of the first slips on a long, precipitous, and dangerous slope. At the close of World War II, Uncle Sam launched Project Shamrock, an intelligence-gathering operation that collected international telegrams through Western Union, RCA Global, and others without warrants. The stated purpose of the program was to search for evidence of espionage and Soviet spying. It would continue for thirty years, well into the 1970s.

The National Security Agency was established in 1952 by then-President Harry Truman. It was an organization so secret that, until it was revealed by the Senate in 1975, insiders in the intelligence community gave it the half-silly, half-sinister nickname "No Such Agency." The revelations that

---

[1] It's also interesting to note that privacy itself, as understood in the modern West, is a surprisingly modern concept. In the US, the modern concept of privacy arose in step with the explosion in newspaper readership over the course of the nineteenth century.

came out were stunning. The NSA's director at the time, General Lew Allen, stated that the NSA maintained extensive watch lists with hundreds of names, and many of the Americans on these lists had their phone lines monitored to gather any evidence of foreign connections and dissidence (particularly antiwar activists), as well as evidence of drug trafficking or potential assassins. This snooping had occurred despite the Supreme Court's earlier decision ruling warrants were required for all domestic intelligence surveillance in 1973.[2] The Senate was at odds here. It believed there were valid arguments for some of this surveillance, but that the surveillance also posed an enormous threat to civil liberties. This investigation, and its conclusions, led directly to the 1978 Foreign Intelligence Surveillance Act, or FISA. In theory, this meant that authorities would need to request a warrant before wiretapping someone, requiring a judge (or panel of judges) to weigh the merits of an intrusion on those sacred Fourth Amendment rights. In practice, however, the secret FISA court rubber stamps the majority of requests. In some cases, surveillance can begin before a warrant is actually issued.

At around the same time, the FBI created a secret counterintelligence program of its own, called—in a burst of creativity—Counterintelligence Program, or COINTELPRO for short.[3] This program, which began in 1956 and ran until at least 1971, was originally meant to combat communist activity within the United States. Over time, the initiative expanded to surveil and disrupt any activities, individuals, or groups thought to be a threat to national security—in practice, this became a blank check to attack anything that might be seen as a threat to the status quo, whether that threat was the Ku Klux Klan, secessionist groups, or civil rights activists like Dr. Martin Luther King Jr. This program, which regularly engaged in techniques Congress deemed "intolerable in a democratic society even if all of

---

[2] *US v. US District Court.*

[3] Read more about COINTELPRO's role in monitoring activists in chapter 6, "Coups and Assassinations."

the targets had been involved in violent activity"[4] was, itself, discovered as the result of a crime. In 1971, a group called the Citizens' Commission to Investigate the FBI broke into a small FBI field office in Media, Pennsylvania, obtained hard evidence of COINTELPRO activities, and leaked these documents to the press. As more information about COINTELPRO and related surveillance programs came to light, it became clear that government agencies were not just breaking laws but repeating the sins of past authorities, especially when it came to disproportionately surveilling people of color (a problem that continues, largely unchanged, in the modern day through facial recognition and good old-fashioned racial profiling). Today, millions of documents pertaining to the program's activities remain unreleased, and much of what the public has been able to see is heavily redacted.

It became clear that government agencies were not just breaking laws but repeating the sins of past authorities.

This is the rough history of surveillance in the US, up to a certain point. And, upon examination, it may seem the facts don't line up with the bizarre claims of that uber-paranoid stereotype we mentioned at the beginning. But this is far from the whole story of government surveillance. That story, a tale of vast overreach, conspiracy, law-breaking, and lack of consequence, is still unfolding today.

You see, while many Americans were scandalized by the existence and activities of the NSA, they weren't aware of a much older, international conspiracy, one that dates back to the height of World War II—an alliance with a name straight out of a Tolkien novel: the Five Eyes.[5]

---

[4] From the US Senate Select Committee to Study Governmental Operations with Respect to Intelligence Activities, informally known as the Church Committee, in 1975.

[5] Sadly not related to the popular burger chain Five Guys . . . so far as we know.

FIVE EYES TO WATCH THEM ALL

AS ALLIES FIGHTING TOGETHER IN WORLD WAR II, the United States and the United Kingdom worked closely to gather and share intelligence through the 1941 Atlantic Charter, articulating Allied goals for the post-war world. This collaboration worked like a charm, so well, in fact, that the countries agreed to continue this relationship after the war, beginning with the UKUSA Agreement of 1946. By 1955, the agreement was formalized to include Canada, Australia, and New Zealand. And thus, far from the public eye, one of the world's most pervasive spying organizations had just been born. Five Eyes (FVEY) presented enormous opportunities for all entities involved, and only expanded throughout the Cold War. The US, in collaboration with the other Five Eyes countries, created the massive ECHELON surveillance network in the 1960s (formally established in 1971) to monitor communications between the Soviet Union and the Eastern Bloc. As with many surveillance programs on the very edge of legality, the program experienced near-constant mission creep,[6] expanding its scope into a global system capable of intercepting private and commercial communications through mass surveillance. Internal leaks dogged the agreement for decades, with notable whistleblowers emerging throughout the 1970s, '80s, and '90s. NSA analyst Perry Fellwock, writing under a pseudonym, first revealed the UKUSA Agreement in 1972. In 1988 a Lockheed employee named Margaret Newsham revealed the existence of ECHELON. Throughout it all, the US denied any knowledge of its existence. In 2013, a

---

[6] Mission creep is an unofficial term for the tendency of projects or initiatives with a narrow, specified focus to gradually expand their scope over time. While the term comes from the world of government projects and military operations, it's a common concept in almost any sphere of business.

whistleblower named Edward Snowden provided inarguable evidence confirming ECHELON. The leaks he disclosed revealed that ECHELON was a subprogram of a larger initiative called FROSTING. FROSTING, it turns out, had been established back in 1966. It had two subprograms: ECHELON, which monitored satellite transmissions from the Intelsat company, and TRANSIENT, which specifically monitored Soviet satellite transmissions. Over the decades, this web of programs transformed into the world's most comprehensive global surveillance system—some of the more extreme estimates reckoned ECHELON and Five Eyes were capable of monitoring up to 90 percent of all the activity on the internet.

Additionally, the Snowden leaks provided a never-before seen glimpse into the inner workings of the NSA, confirming two types of data collection: the PRISM program and upstream collection. PRISM, now generally known as downstream surveillance, involves the collection of communication from large, private tech firms—the Googles, Facebooks, and Yahoos of the world. Upstream surveillance focuses on collecting communications as they travel across the backbone of the internet. The operations are extremely powerful, comprehensive, and, for a long time, had very little in the way of substantive oversight. In both cases, the intelligence community can target any foreign person located outside of the US who is suspected of having "foreign intelligence information." *What exactly is "foreign intelligence information"?* you may ask. That's the tricky, brilliant part. Intelligence agencies have a secret definition for the term, but it's believed to be incredibly broad. So broad, in fact, that agencies could easily target journalists reporting on foreign governments, or businesses and entrepreneurs working in the private sector that are seeking to expand their operations to new countries.

The laws that require private tech entities to turn over relevant information also prohibit them from telling their users that the data has been handed over. In the case of upstream surveillance, NSA telecom partners tap directly into the high-capacity fiber optic cables that carry online traffic and copy the data flowing through those cables. In theory, the data then undergoes a filtration process, getting rid of any communication deemed to be "wholly domestic."

As far as anyone can tell, it hasn't stopped. At this point, any reasonable person might point out that this seems to be a violation of the Fourth Amendment. This is where an insidious loophole comes into play: while the US may be restricted (in theory) from monitoring the domestic population without warrants or probable cause, other members of Five Eyes can monitor that domestic activity to the best of their ability, and then share the information with the US, meaning the US didn't technically acquire the information. Additionally, the US can monitor contact between a person residing in the US and an individual in a foreign country.

Today Five Eyes is generally understood to engage in multiple types of intelligence gathering. Their strategies include scooping up as much available data as possible from the internet and telecommunications networks for later analysis. You don't have to be a suspected criminal to come under scrutiny. The nature of the arrangement means this intelligence organization doesn't appear to answer to the laws of its own member countries, and all signs indicate there's no chance of it going away anytime soon.

NSA: THE WAR ON TERROR

IN THE WAKE OF THE ATTACKS ON SEPTEMBER 11, 2001, the NSA was given the green light to massively expand. On September 25, then-Department of Justice legal counsel John Yoo wrote a memo claiming the president had the authority to approve antiterrorism tactics up to and including warrantless wiretapping if doing so is deemed vital for national security. On October 26 of the same year, Congress passed the USA Patriot

Act, officially granting Uncle Sam much more latitude in acquiring wiretapping warrants. This was framed as a way for the government to respond more quickly to threats. Critics argued it would ultimately be used in an inappropriate manner. By 2021 most of these critics would have good reason to believe they were correct. In the two decades after the September 11 attacks, the Patriot Act was continually reauthorized until ultimately expiring under the Trump administration. However, with the lid off Pandora's jar, it's safe to say there's no real way, at this point, to take back the massive state spying infrastructure and powerful technology the act unleashed.

While they may not be targeting you specifically, the government's secret surveillance programs are almost certainly monitoring you. Experts generally believe ECHELON is not a real-time tapping network. Instead, it scrapes as much information as it can, then later sifts through this gigantic morass of data for keywords or other activity intelligence services deem to be "suspicious." If necessary, the entirety of your life online can be pulled up, and thanks to cooperation from telecom companies and the tech industry through FISA and the PRISM program, authorities can also glean a lot of information about your life off the net, including where you go, what you do, whom you do it with, and where you spend money. For some, this is all well and good. "I'm not doing anything wrong," the reasoning goes. "So what do I care if the NSA knows just how much I like to skim Reddit? Does the government really agonize over whether I remembered to get my library books in on time?"

There are serious problems with this perspective.

First, you can't knowledgeably consent to give over your data when you have little idea about how, when, or why it will be used in the future. In cases concerning both private social media entities and government surveillance agencies, the collection of your data can also, in practice, include the collection of data from other people you've come into contact with, whether or not they consent. Dragnet-style operations vacuuming up every conceivable bit of information can also quickly become a version of the old Six Degrees of Kevin Bacon game. The leaks by Edward Snowden confirmed that the NSA has been collecting metadata from phone calls and internet activity for years, with the willing assistance of telecommunications companies. (Yes, Tinfoil Hat Guy, it turns out there is indeed something big, a real conspiracy with a multitude of players involved.) Experts believe there's not currently a way for intelligence agencies to capture every piece of online traffic and store it, but collecting the metadata—time stamps, email subject lines, IP addresses, and so on—is a more viable strategy. If the information collected falls into a certain predetermined pattern, the agency can decide to dive deeper, collecting all the associated content. Additionally, this initial collection of metadata alone allows the NSA to argue they're not really "reading" personal information. In court, the agency has argued metadata comes with no expectation of privacy; it's like reading the addresses written on an envelope, instead of opening it to read the letter within.

The analysis of the data collected by these agencies is largely automated, so it's not as if there's some hapless army of interns tucked away in a data center scrolling the world's emails one subject line at a time, or meticulously, manually transcribing every single phone conversation across the entirety of the planet. But the algorithms conducting this search do, in a way, pay homage to the Kevin Bacon game. As they sort through these mountains of data, they build upon knowledge of preexisting connections and become capable of determining how many "hops" or "degrees" one person is from another. You could, in theory, use this system to determine how far away a given person is from being directly connected to Kevin Bacon. You could take the same person and see how connected they are to Osama Bin Laden. The NSA states that it looks at between two to three hops from a given subject. If you have a direct relationship with a terrorist, criminal, or other target, that's considered a "one-hop" relationship. This means there's a solid line directly connecting you to that person on the NSA's relationship graph. You may not have known of this person's nefarious activities, but at some point you called each other, you emailed them, or perhaps visited their website. The pattern can extend further—you may not have directly contacted a criminal, but let's say you've talked with, emailed, or become Facebook friends with someone who has. You're officially two hops away from the target, which means your data is also up for grabs. At the far end of the NSA's admitted strategy, you could have simply been in contact with someone who was in contact with someone who was in contact with the target, making you three hops away and still, so far as the agency is concerned, fair game.

SIX DEGREES OF KEVIN BACON

Created in 1994 by three friends from Albright College who were snowed in one night watching movies that all seemed to have Kevin Bacon in them, this pop culture parlor game requires players to take an arbitrarily chosen actor and connect them through mutual costars in other films to Kevin Bacon in six steps or fewer. (Currently, the average "Bacon Number" is roughly 3.2.) Interestingly, Kevin Bacon is only the 577th best person to use as the centerpiece of a Hollywood game like this. The best would be the late Christopher Lee, the English actor who starred in more than 200 films over a seventy-year career.

The game's a fun diversion for film buffs, but eerily similar to the disconcerting practice used in some surveillance programs, which is anchored in this idea that all people are six or fewer degrees of separation from each other. If you consider that the average Facebook or Instagram user has roughly 200 friends or followers, and you extend that net out exponentially (i.e., your 200 friends each have 200 friends each of whom have 200 friends), by the sixth step you are at 64 trillion. That number is nearly 550 times greater than the number of people who have ever lived. Which means, even when you remove all the people not online or with no social media presence (50 percent of whom live with someone who does), you've still gotten to everyone multiple times.

*all Bacon bits of trivia come from OracleOfBacon.org

If you fall within that three-hop space, algorithms may flag you and your data for more in-depth analysis, meaning you may be the subject of a warrant request from the secret FISA court. If approved, this request will allow the NSA to use PRISM to access anything they can get on you. Internet companies are legally required to hand over any data on you from their servers if it falls in that three-hop range. This means *everything.* Literally any information that could be deemed relevant. Additionally, your current online activity will be subject to more scrutiny. The NSA has multiple internet taps and can use these to track you, searching to determine what you may or may not know about the target's activities, goals, or upcoming crimes. Because the warrant is secret, you do not have to be informed of this activity. And there's another problem: thanks to the way social media platforms and online communication are structured, it's laughably easy for you to be within two to three degrees of separation from any number of people, many of whom you may have never heard of, let alone communicated with directly. Back in 2013, as the Snowden revelations hit the mainstream, the UK-based *Telegraph* came up with some scary math: the average person, they found, has 190 Facebook connections, which could be considered first-hop folks, actual friends.[7] If that individual is considered a person of interest, their 190 friends also get further scrutiny. When you progress to a second hop, that pool of associations explodes to 31,046 people, all of whom the NSA could theoretically be allowed to spy on. Take it one step further to the third hop and you're looking at easily more than 5 million friends of friends of friends, and the NSA can likewise scoop up any data they wish on them. The population of the United States is just over 328 million people. In 2016, Facebook reported that its then-1.6 billion users were connected by an average of 3.57 degrees. With these two pieces of information, it would take fewer than one hundred people at the right social/communicative position

---

[7] Of course, there's a difference between "Facebook friends" and real friends, but that's a story for another day.

to green-light the in-depth surveillance of every single US resident, as they would be about three hops away through one communication channel or another.[8] This may seem like overkill, especially considering a great many people might not know whom they've been associated with—after all, we can't realistically control our friends' activities on the phone or online, and most of us would be downright offended if our friends and loved ones tried to do the same to us.

So, what happens if you get flagged? If you live in the US, the NSA then passes on this information to the FBI. And whether or not you've been flagged, your international communications are already up for grabs. Calling an old friend from your days abroad in Paris? Fair game. Communicating via email with coworkers in Australia, Chile, or any other country? That communication is up for grabs as well. Many see this as an egregious violation of personal rights, and that's because, well, it is.

Advocates for the security state believe our government's surveillance strategy is necessary, regardless of the privacy issues it raises.

Advocates for the security state believe our government's surveillance strategy is necessary, regardless of the privacy issues it raises. While it may not be entirely ethical, and while it flies in the face of the rights guaranteed in the Fourth Amendment, it is even more unethical, they argue, to hesitate from doing whatever possible to save lives. However, that line of reasoning often fails to acknowledge the inevitable errors, missteps, and misfires that will occur with any operation at this scale. The Privacy and

---

[8] Here's some terrifying, cocktail napkin math: if one person can result in 5 million third-hop candidates, it would take fewer than 66 individuals to create a pool of 328 million third-hop candidates in total, which is roughly equal to the population of the entire United States. Luckily, this is oversimplified, as there would doubtlessly be a lot of "repeat" connections in the system.

Civil Liberties Oversight Board, part of the executive branch, went so far as to imply this mass-surveillance apparatus might not actually be worth the effort, noting that the bulk collection of telephone records appeared to produce "little unique value," and seemed, for the most part, to be duplicating more targeted techniques. When courts ruled the system was responsible for persistent, clear violations of privacy, the NSA eventually closed down at least two other surveillance tools, which, more than anything, implies that following the rules was costlier than whatever intelligence value the programs may have presented.

Another fact that's not often brought up in these conversations: How secure is the NSA itself? After all, doesn't the magnitude of the Snowden leak prove the NSA's own treasure trove of techniques and data is itself vulnerable? What happens if a foreign adversary worms its way into this orchard of illicit information? If a single employee—a contractor, specifically—can pull off a heist that shakes the foundation of the entire applecart, what could a motivated nation-state with billions in cash and its own well-established spying apparatus pull off? And what would it be able to do with all that information once it obtained it?

There's a second issue at play here: Who decides what makes a person a "bad guy"? What if you haven't broken any laws but support causes that seem ideologically opposed to future leadership? The algorithms themselves obey no moral code, any more than a gun and a bullet pick their target; they simply carry out their function or, in this case, their programming. The people pointing the system at a given target become the ultimate arbiters of later actions. Say, for example, a new administration is cracking down on civil rights, and you're a member of a group organizing sit-ins and protests. It doesn't matter that these protests are nonviolent, that all the required permits are in place, and so on. Every official box can be checked, every bureaucratic i dotted, every housekeeping t crossed for your demonstration. Nevertheless, the legal right of the government to spy on your communications will remain. If you or your associates are perceived to be a potentially disruptive force, you can and will be monitored. And given the secrecy surrounding these surveillance processes, completely innocent people may, without their knowledge, be placed on a watch list; subjected to literally unwarranted, intense scrutiny; profiled; and discriminated against all in the name of a greater good. Critics contend that the racial, ethnic, and religious biases of older surveillance programs remain in full effect in the new online version of Orwell's *1984*, and they have the receipts to prove it. People of Asian descent, people of color, and Muslims have all been disproportionately targeted by this leviathan of digital snooping.

All the above becomes profoundly dangerous when we consider the implications toward political opponents—rival politicians, for example, or activist leaders like the next Martin Luther King. So long as the NSA works in secrecy with little transparency or meaningful oversight, the forces in control of government will have the opportunity to use these enormous monitoring capabilities against political foes. Through threats, intimidation, and harassment, an election may be over well before it begins. To some this may sound like the dystopian narrative of an authoritarian dictatorship. To others, some version of these scenarios is already happening, every day, on a level undreamed of by most Americans. And there's no tinfoil that can stop it.

With all this in mind, what can we say about the future of mass surveillance? Knowing that this all-seeing eye is at once capable, growing, and active, what can an ordinary person do to protect themselves?

Well, you could go off the grid. Never touch the internet or a smartphone again. Close all your credit cards, pay all your debts, liquidate your assets into piles of cash and gold bars, and live out in the wild. Some people have taken this route. However, it's not possible for most people, even if they wanted to do it. Family ties, social and financial obligations, the primal urge for contact with fellow human beings—these and other factors converge to make the life of a wilderness-loving hermit a pipe dream for the vast majority of people in the US.

And it should go without saying that the vast majority of people aren't supervillains from some James Bond novel. Most people aren't slipping away in the dark of night to plot the downfall of civilization, even when they realize there are aspects of modern life that could inarguably be improved. Most people tend to want the same basic things: an expectation of safety for themselves and their loved ones. Food, shelter, access to clean water, economic and educational opportunities. A chance, even if not a guarantee, to provide a better life for their children.[9]

A surveillance state creates a positive feedback loop, becoming an ouroboros of ever-increasing powers and ever-eroding rights. We are only at the beginning of how technology will expand government spying powers. The increasing role of unmanned aerial vehicles (UAVs) and drones can bring real-time visual surveillance to the streets, the same way it's occurring with traffic cameras and some CCTV systems today. And the obsessive monitoring doesn't necessarily stop at your front door. The popularization of in-home smart devices can function as real-time audio monitoring devices, eavesdropping on private conversations at home. In 2017, the *Washington Post* revealed the US government has already turned theoretical exploits and vulnerabilities into functioning attack tools. One of these goes by the name Weeping Angel.

Weeping Angel, designed to target Samsung smart TVs, would allow the government to place televisions in a "fake off" mode, at which point it would use the television's microphone and internet connection to send recordings of conversations to a CIA server.

The existence of real government programs allowing them to spy on you inside your own home takes us well past the realm of theory. And the problem with discovering surveillance programs is similar to the problem of eradicating cockroaches in your home: for every one you discover, it's reasonable to assume there are others lurking in the shadows. Given

---

[9]   The Founding Fathers of the US cleverly referred to this as "the pursuit of happiness"—meaning that while not everyone may achieve their goals, they are more than welcome to give it their best shot.

that technology eternally outpaces legislation, it's reasonable to assume America's political leadership and general public will continually be playing catch-up in the surveillance game for the foreseeable future.

The next step, which is distressingly, increasingly plausible, is one of *predictive, preemptive* action, the idea that a government agency might leverage its newfound powers of analysis and observation toward prognostication. We are not too far away from a scenario wherein probabilities may be conflated with probable cause. What happens when an intelligence apparatus decides that it can take action based on probabilities? Let's say that, according to some arcane, classified algorithm, this hypothetical system calculates there is a more than 50 percent chance a person may be involved in an upcoming protest or demonstration the rulers of a country would rather not see come to pass. Will that probability be enough to have the person detained, their personal information pored over? If more than 50 percent probability isn't enough, then what would that threshold be? Ninety percent? Eighty percent? Seventy percent? Fifty-one percent?

Civilization isn't there yet. But with our legal barriers weakened and our technology powerful and unfettered, it's safe to say that things are about to get uglier than ever before.

CHAPTER FOUR

UFOS

IMAGINE CAMPING LATE IN THE EVENING, NEAR A RIVER ALONG AN ISOLATED STRETCH OF WOODS. The sky above you shines clear, deep, and endless. You can see stars and constellations in breathtaking detail. Some stars shine brighter than others. Some twinkle. A few lights move lazily through the distance—satellites, you muse, or maybe planes. You're not an expert on these things, yet you can appreciate the aesthetic of the cosmos all the same.

And then it happens. Something much faster than a plane, much closer than a star, appears. It hovers. You see a number of lights, but the shape is unfamiliar. You fumble for your phone, holding it up to record—and you grab just a few seconds of shaky footage before the thing moves away. Whether you consider yourself a dyed-in-the-wool skeptic or a true believer in all things officially unexplained, you have just seen a UFO.

illions of people believe they've experienced something like this, sometimes alone, sometimes in groups.[1] The vast majority of people who've seen a UFO aren't nutcases or eccentrics. They're people from all walks of life, in pretty much every imaginable demographic. For many, the experience becomes just another fascinating, fun anecdote to share with friends and loved ones. Others may find themselves galvanized, inspired to dig deeper into the various reports, amateur and official, about mysterious objects and phenomena in the sky. Still others may not share their experience at all, as they become afraid this may affect their credibility or social standing.

After all, not everyone would immediately tell their boss, "Holy smokes, I saw a UFO!" Odds are you could become the "crazy coworker," the one who believes in aliens. And you definitely don't want to confess to seeing a UFO if you are a public figure. Stating a belief in UFOs can seriously damage the reputation of a politician or celebrity. Public shaming of people who have seen strange sights in the sky is all too common, partially because people tend to misunderstand a few things about UFOs.

To begin with, UFOs are real. You've probably seen one yourself. This doesn't mean there's some vast, intergalactic conspiracy afoot. The term "UFO" is just shorthand for an Unidentified Flying Object, meaning that anything you see in the sky and fail to conclusively identify is, by definition, a UFO. In most civilian sightings, the UFO turns out to be an unfamiliar aircraft, an atmospheric phenomenon, or, in some cases, a purposeful hoax. Once someone is able to identify the object, it is, by definition, no longer a UFO.

UFOs are often associated with extraterrestrial entities. This should come as no surprise. For thousands of years, human beings have dreamed of being visited by intelligent creatures from somewhere beyond the bounds of Earth—a cosmic counterpart, proof that we are not alone in the

---

[1] The National UFO Reporting Center (US) has collected over 135,000 reports of UFO sightings since 1905. The majority of these sightings occurred between the years 2000 and 2021.

great emptiness of this particular universe. While the sheer size of the universe makes a solid argument that some form of intelligent life may have existed in the past, may exist now, or will exist at some point in the future, that same problem of size virtually guarantees human beings will not meet these entities.[2]

Still, there's something comforting in the idea that we are not alone. It's terrifying to imagine that we are the only inhabited planet in the vastness of the cosmos. It's easy to understand why so many people feel like Fox Mulder, the fictional FBI agent from *The X-Files*: we want to believe.

So, yes: UFOs are real. Unfortunately for the sci-fi fans in the crowd, this isn't the same thing as saying "aliens are real," any more than seeing an Elvis cover band is the same thing as seeing Elvis Presley (who has, by the way, very much left the building).[3] Most people would be hard-pressed to identify a specific model of commercial airplane, much less distinguish between various types of fighter jets, so it's no surprise that there are so many reports of UFOs in general. Most of us just don't have the education or experience required to successfully identify things we see at such great distance, for mere minutes or moments at a time.

And we've had a lot of time to think about this conundrum. Early *Homo sapiens* likely studied the mysteries of stars in much the same way a modern city-dweller does today, if they venture past conurbations into the wilderness at night. (In fact, there's a compelling argument that early humans may have had more knowledge of the stars than today's average non-astronomer, as they lived without large amounts of light pollution.) On

---

[2]   This dilemma is best encapsulated by the Fermi Paradox. Named after Nobel Prize-winning physicist Enrico Fermi, the paradox hinges on the lack of evidence for intelligent extraterrestrial life. Given the size and age of the universe, the estimated number of stars with habitable planets, the odds of sentient life developing and so on, there's a statistical argument that hundreds of civilizations should have popped up far before the rise of humanity, and left some sort of evidence of their existence. Yet no evidence has been found. As Fermi famously said during a lunch with colleagues in 1950: "So? Where is everybody?"

[3]   Soon after Elvis Presley's death on August 16, 1977, rumors spread that the King of Rock and Roll had faked his death, and was in hiding.

a clear night, the staggering view of the cosmos can make the universe feel impossibly large and, depending on your mood, can be either fundamentally depressing or profoundly inspiring. As you read this, tens of thousands of people are actively searching the sky for signs of life unfamiliar to this planet. Some are astronomers and astrophysicists. Some are amateur investigators and kids with their first telescope. Some are government agents.

That's the modern wrinkle, a relatively recent development in the millennia-old reports of UFOs. Despite multiple statements to the contrary, the modern US government—and other governments throughout the world—has been deeply interested in the UFO phenomenon for almost a century. Various administrations lied about this interest and openly dismissed various reports as hogwash. And while they were doing this in the public sphere, they were often using taxpayer money to finance extensive, secret searches of their own. As conspiratorial as it may sound, Uncle Sam has actively been searching for UFOs—and they still don't know how to explain everything they've found.

PROJECT BLUE BOOK

GENERAL CONSPIRACY THEORISTS AND UFOLOGISTS have long had an overlapping, close relationship. Their interests align in a common belief: the government knows something about UFOs and conspires to keep this secret. It's a fascinating Venn diagram, and true to a disturbing degree. The US Air Force's initial investigation of UFOs began in 1948, known as Project Sign.[4] Later the name was changed to Project Grudge, and in 1953 it became Project Blue Book. Between 1948 and 1969, the US Air Force

---

[4]   Funny story, Project Sign was initially called Project Saucer, but that must have been a little too on the nose for Uncle Sam.

investigated 12,618 reported sightings. Of these total sightings, 11,917 were found to have been caused by material objects (such as balloons, satellites, and aircraft), immaterial objects (such as lightning, reflections, and other natural phenomena), astronomical objects (such as stars, planets, and the sun and moon), weather conditions, and hoaxes. Only 701 reported sightings remained unexplained. The entirety of the project was heavily classified—and the secrecy here was an impressive feat all its own. The operations were conducted primarily due to concerns that earthly, rather than extraterrestrial, rivals might possess an edge in aerospace technology. The official conclusion of Project Blue Book, since declassified, reads like a careful rebuke of those looking for "little green men."

"No UFO reported, investigated, and evaluated by the Air Force," the report noted, "has ever given any indication of threat to our national security." It continues, "There has been no evidence submitted to or discovered by the Air Force that sightings categorized as 'unidentified' present technological developments or principles beyond the range of present day scientific knowledge." Additionally, the report concludes that, despite being unable to conclusively explain hundreds of sightings, "There has been no evidence indicating that sightings categorized as 'unidentified' are extraterrestrial vehicles."

These quotations provide a clear and troubling peek behind the curtain of government. Remember, this investigation took place as the Cold War was ramping up to unprecedented heights. The US and its primary geopolitical rival, the USSR, spent untold billions of dollars searching to learn more about their opponents' capabilities while also working around the clock to develop new weapons of war. The conflict was further complicated by each side's extensive, sometimes bizarre attempts at misinformation and propaganda. The USSR was more than happy to spread information indicating it had massive, secret weapons—even when these stories were highly embellished, or outright false. The US was also more than happy to tacitly encourage overblown news stories of aliens and flying saucers, as these reports could provide cover for active classified projects, such as the construction of next-generation spy planes and global monitoring of nuclear activity (more on that later).

So while outsiders might think Blue Book looks like an investigation into little green men, the government saw it more as a secret search to make sure they were not outclassed by enemy forces. This was a very real concern, and one that rightly terrified military leaders. If you don't know what your enemy has up its sleeve, you can't plan to defend against it. If you can't maintain control of your own airspace, then you logically have no defense against what may enter it, such as conventional missiles or, in the worst-case scenario, nuclear weapons.

Before the so-called age of transparency and sunshine laws (see chapter 8 for more), there was little ethical concern about this deception. Legislators and the military alike assumed—correctly—that the USSR had spies both in the halls of government and in the general civilian/business population, meaning that anything the average citizen knew would also be known to the Soviets, and when combined with reports from other well-placed assets, that public knowledge might assist them in piecing together increasing sophisticated understandings of secret US activity. The decision seemed simple. While lying to the American public may not be the best move in the world, it was still the right thing to do for the greater good.

The CIA openly admitted the extent of this practice in a study called *CIA's Role in the Study of UFOs, 1947–90*, which was originally published in a secret agency journal called *Studies of Intelligence*. In 1992, the CIA began releasing unclassified versions of the journal. This report, which appears in the 1997 edition, is freely available online today. While it may feel like a letdown for folks convinced aliens exist, it provides an invaluable perspective on the government's rationale for lying to so many people, so successfully, for such a long stretch of time.

The author, Gerald K. Haines, writes that the US Air Force knew people weren't making up these sightings. In fact, it was common knowledge that most reports by ordinary civilians and aviation experts from the 1950s on were based on short glimpses of secret spy planes like the SR-71 or the

U-2. These planes had capabilities that would have astonished the public at the time. They were black projects, meaning they did not officially exist. (Projects like this continue in the modern day.) Both planes flew at extremely high altitudes, and didn't look like commercial airliners, which could then fly only to altitudes of about 30,000 feet maximum. In stark contrast, the U-2 could double that altitude, cruising comfortably at more than 60,000 feet. The SR-71 went even higher, hitting an altitude of 80,000 feet. It wasn't a genuine interstellar craft, and its pilot was human, but it was surprisingly similar to some of the wilder conjectures of UFO fans. The two-person crew even had to wear pressurized flight suits. Had an SR-71 landed outside a military base, these guys would have looked like astronauts. Or, just maybe, aliens.

SR-71 BLACKBIRD

Today we recognize the SR-71 Blackbird as the antecedent to the Stealth aircraft family, but in the 1960s when it was developed out of the Lockheed Skunk Works in Palmdale, California, it was unlike anything the world had ever seen. It was 107 feet long—almost ten feet longer than a massive C-130 transport plane. It was basically all black (the paint was actually dark blue) and made almost completely from titanium, which the US sourced surreptitiously from its Cold War enemy, the Soviet Union, through dummy corporations and allies in developing nations. It used a special fuel and nitrogen in its tires. It flew as high as sixteen miles up at more than three times the speed of sound. It could outrun surface-to-air missiles (which it did on more than one occasion) and it still holds the record for fastest military aircraft, nearly sixty years after its first flight. Oh, and it had no guns, only cameras. And despite all that, none of the 20 aircraft that were commissioned (32 were built, 12 were lost in accidents) and would ultimately fly thousands of missions were shot down.

It's important to note these planes weren't built for fighting; instead of missiles or bombs, they carried highly sensitive electronic gear, meant to snoop on enemy radio and radar transmissions. Both were conceived by the CIA, developed by the Lockheed Corporation, and usually flown by the US Air Force. While the CIA and the USAF had had their share of differences in the past, they could agree on at least one thing: the public could not know the truth about these planes.

And so the stories began. The US Air Force actively fed reporters and the public tales of atmospheric phenomena as a distraction from the true subjects of multiple sightings. That mysterious shape you saw, floating northward like a ghost? That was a temperature inversion, or ice crystals—it's not your fault for being confused. You're not a meteorologist, after all . . . but your story is easily dismissed.

UFOs are real. The US government knew this, because it was literally manufacturing, maintaining, and flying them. And yes, the government lied about this.

Privately, those in the know obsessed over these reports and kept close tabs on them, correlating them to known reconnaissance flights. The study notes: "Over half of all UFO reports from the late 1950s through the 1960s were accounted for by manned reconnaissance flights," explaining that this "led the Air Force to make misleading and deceptive statements to the public in order to allay public fears and to protect an extraordinarily sensitive national security project."

When this grand deception came to light, it fed public distrust. What if this revelation was itself a diversionary tactic, another strategy of deceit? This doubt, which is doubtlessly well founded, continues in the modern day. In fact, it's only deepened, and strengthened, as similar programs come to light.

At least part of the conspiracy theory here is true. UFOs are real. The US government knew this, because it was literally manufacturing, maintaining, and flying them. And yes, the government lied about this. So how did it manage to keep such a grand conspiracy, with so many players, a secret for so long? To some, the answer isn't a matter of shredded documents and manila folders stamped SECRET. Instead, it's a matter of on-the-ground human contact, another secret program meant to intimidate and suppress witnesses, by any means necessary. This belief is best summed up in three words: Men in Black.

MEN IN BLACK

LET'S GO BACK TO OUR EARLIER EXAMPLE. You're camping, it's late at night, and you've just experienced the most bizarre event of your life. You're convinced what you saw was not some normal plane, nor aurora borealis, nor a trick of perspective. You are certain you saw *something*—and though you didn't get the best video of it, you do have video. You have proof of what you saw. You're out in the boonies, miles from civilization, but you still have a signal on your phone. You send the video to some friends or family members, telling them what happened. You don't feel like sleeping, but you try to get some shut-eye before breaking camp and heading home.

The next day, you get a knock on your door. Two men are standing on your porch, dressed in black, nondescript, slightly outdated suits. Behind them, parked or idling on the street, you see an older-model car. It looks like something out of a black-and-white film.

"May we come in," say the men, calling you by name, with a tone that lets you know this isn't really a question. Startled, you step back and open the door wide. You've just met the Men in Black.

The concept of Men in Black—mysterious plainclothes agents who appear in the wake of UFO sightings—remains one of the most popular pieces of conspiratorial UFO folklore. It's referenced in countless works of fiction and has become the basis for a film franchise. As conspiracies go, it's mostly false. The origin of the tale can be traced back to a specific series of events in July 1947.

A guy named Harold Dahl and his son Charles, along with their dog, were on a conservation mission near the eastern shore of Maury Island on the Puget Sound when they encountered what they perceived as six donut-shaped objects hovering a half mile above their boat. Dahl claimed he watched as one of the discs fluttered to earth and disintegrated, showering his boat with fragments, some of which killed his dog. Dahl reportedly took photographs of these objects, later presenting them to his supervisor, Fred Crisman. Crisman later visited the scene himself and saw a strange object in the sky. He believed it to be an aircraft. Dahl later claimed that he was visited by a mysterious man in black the next morning. This guy wasn't immediately sinister—in fact, he took Dahl out for breakfast. But in conversation, he appeared to know exactly what Dahl had experienced, in surprising detail, and cryptically warned Dahl not to speak about the incident, lest there be complications. He allegedly told Dahl, "What I have said is proof to you that I know a great deal more about this experience of yours than you will want to believe." The US investigated this incident, resulting in a memorandum titled "Project Saucer." Their conclusion? It was all a prank. They note the report occurred just a few days after a man named Kenneth Arnold claimed to see multiple "crescent-shaped" craft floating around Mount Rainier, a story that generated massive regional and national interest.[5]

According to the memo, Crisman and Dahl may have had a financial motive. They immediately tried to sell their story to an adventure magazine

---

[5] Despite the fact that Arnold described the craft as crescent in shape, his report became the catalyst for a surge of reports on "flying saucers" during 1947.

based in Chicago. The magazine contacted Kenneth Arnold, who traveled to Tacoma with a pilot from United Airlines, one Captain Emil J. Smith. Smith, by the way, had also spent some time in the UFO spotlight, as he'd reported seeing disc-shaped craft over Boise, Idaho, earlier the same year, on the Fourth of July. While in Tacoma, Arnold contacted two army intelligence officers for help investigating the claim. The men met in secret at the Winthrop Hotel in Tacoma, where Dahl produced samples of the fragments he said came from the disc. The two officers left the next day on a B-25 bound for Hamilton Field, California, taking some fragments with them for further analysis.

Another strange twist: the plane they took crashed, killing both officers en route. The other two passengers, a crew chief and a "hitchhiker," parachuted to safety. Not long after this crash, newspapers and wire services around Tacoma began receiving anonymous phone calls claiming the fallen B-25 had been purposely shot from the air with a 20mm cannon. Some papers darkly hinted the plane had been destroyed because of those fragments aboard, though the government maintains a thorough investigation of the accident found no indication of foul play.[6]

On the same day this plane crashed, Dahl and Crisman took Captain Smith to see the boat that had allegedly been damaged by the falling fragments of a destroyed UFO. Smith wasn't particularly impressed, later telling investigators that while he could see recent repairs to the windshield and lights of the craft, it didn't look like the damage could have been caused by the events they described in their story.

And here's the kicker: under later questioning, Dahl and Crisman reversed their stories, claiming it was all a hoax. The fragments they'd presented as proof were just unusual rock formations found on Maury Island, and they'd hoped including the fragments could increase their odds of selling the story to that magazine in Chicago. Still, the match of speculation

---

[6] The memo notes the following explanation for the crash: "The crash was caused by a burned exhaust stack which in turn caught the left wing afire. The blazing wing broke from the fuselage and tore off the plane's tail."

had already been applied to a conspiracy powder keg, creating the folklore we know today.

As for the rise of the Men in Black? That didn't really take off until almost a decade later, when an author named Gray Barker recounted Dahl's Men in Black story in his 1956 book *They Knew Too Much about Flying Saucers.* By then the government considered Dahl's story thoroughly debunked—at least, if you believe the official reports—but the idea of shadowy government agents was just too juicy not to catch on. Barker played a pivotal role in this, as his book connects Dahl's story about a "man in a black suit" with another story from a guy named Albert K. Bender, who claimed that three men dressed in a similar fashion visited him back in 1953.

Before Barker's book hit the press, it's extraordinarily difficult to find references to the Men in Black. At that point, only a few people subscribed to UFO-centered newsletters had heard of Albert K. Bender.

But as the years went by, more and more people claimed to have encountered these Men in Black, and the story evolved. While they were originally believed to be FBI agents, later storytellers would claim they didn't seem entirely human—their speech was stilted, and they used outdated phrases. They looked . . . off, somehow, with glowing eyes or oddly pallid complexions. In 1962, Bender wrote a book of his own, *Flying Saucers and the Three Men.* His description introduces some of the supernatural elements that become so common in later years. For example, he writes the three men "floated about a foot off the floor. . . . They looked like clergymen, but wore hats similar to Homburg style. The faces were not clearly discernible, for the hats partly hid and shaded them. . . . He describes how the "eyes of all three figures suddenly lit up like flashlight bulbs," how they "seemed to burn into my very soul as the pains above my eyes became almost unbearable." Bender also claimed the men who visited him weren't humans at all, but aliens. According to him, they only appeared human because they kidnapped Earthlings and wore their bodies as disguises, an idea later echoed in films like *Dark City.* Bender maintained his version of this story for the rest of his life, up until his death in 2002.

Levitation? Glowing eyes and the ability to cause excruciating headaches with a glance? This doesn't sound like a particularly inconspicuous, or subtle, approach. But with that nitpick aside, there's no denying this was great fodder for Barker's book. Nowadays, scholars and friends of Gray Barker are split on his perceived motives. One old friend, John Sherwood, later claimed that Barker made the Men in Black up as a joke. Barker even speculated, with friends and off the record, that Bender may have simply had a bad dream. If this was indeed the case, Albert K. Bender was very much not in on the joke. He claimed his encounter with the three Men in Black caused him to cancel his forthcoming article on the UFO cover-up, and he suddenly shut down the organization he'd founded, the International Flying Saucer Bureau. This was the first major civilian club for UFO enthusiasts, but it was only a year old.

While Albert K. Bender's claims are both outlandish and unprovable, it seems that he genuinely believed them. However, believing something to be fact doesn't automatically make it so, and a person's individual recollection of a moment or event changes subtly over time. Despite the problems with these initial stories—despite the fact that we know more or less how the Men in Black evolved into a part of UFO folklore—belief in these mysterious entities persists. Why?

For the hardcore believers, each debunked encounter can easily be dismissed as misinformation, disregarded as these conclusions do not support the believers' starting assumption. For more academic investigators, the persistence of Men in Black can be explained by two factors: First, shadowy government agents do exist. They don't have superpowers, and they aren't from some far-flung galactic empire, but there are plainclothes agents aplenty, back then and in the modern day, working directly for government agencies. Knowing this makes the story seem a little less implausible. Second, the idea is regularly retold, reinterpreted, and showcased in popular media. Every time the American public, and the world, encounters another work of fiction centering on the idea of the Men in Black, people begin toying with the story anew. If the wildest stories about

Men in Black were somehow true, it's fair to say they are terrible at their jobs. Why else would so many reports about them exist—aren't they supposed to stop this stuff from getting out?

There's one more factor here, and it's by far the most important piece of the puzzle: while movies like *Men in Black* and TV shows like *The X-Files* kept sinister government agents in the zeitgeist, the US government genuinely was sending people out to investigate stories of UFOs. And just like the case of Project Blue Book, Uncle Sam was yet again conducting these activities in secret. The US government may not believe in "aliens," but it turns out it very much believes in UFOs.

But before we get to that conspiracy, we need to unravel the true story of the world's most famous UFO incident: the Roswell Crash.

ROSWELL

WE CAN'T TALK ABOUT UFOS and conspiracies without mentioning the most well-known UFO incident in conspiracy folklore: the Roswell Crash.

On July 8, 1947—the same month Dahl claimed to encounter the Men in Black—the Roswell Army Airfield sent out a press release announcing it had discovered and acquired the remnants of a "flying disc" from a local ranch. Sometime in late June or early July, *something* crashed in the New Mexican desert. A rancher named W. W. "Mac" Brazel encountered a strange pile of debris on his ranch about eighty miles northwest of Roswell, New Mexico. The ensuing investigation became a circus, with the local and federal government changing their explanation several times. The "flying disc" narrative was quickly retracted, but each change or clarification only gave more fuel to the conspiracy fire. Today official sources maintain the wreckage was part of a top-secret operation called Project Mogul—and given the nature of this project, it was easier for the US Air Force to appear to entertain outlandish stories of aliens and UFOs. In this case, they literally wanted that unidentified, crashed object to remain unidentified. Otherwise, the USSR might have learned too much about experimental US surveillance programs.

In retrospect, it's easy to see the larger context. This had become a bumper year for UFO stories, a time that Uncle Sam would later characterize in internal memos as "the UFO Wave of 1947," beginning with sixteen alleged sightings that occurred between May 17 and July 12.[7] The public had UFOs—and aliens—on the brain. The initial stories both came from a local paper, the *Roswell Daily Record*. The first story hit the headlines on July 8, claiming Major Jesse A. Marcel, the intelligence officer of the 509th Bomb Group (stationed at Roswell Army Airfield) had recovered a "flying disc," and this object had been "flown to higher headquarters." The same article also reported that a local couple had seen a large unidentified object fly by their home on July 2.

By the next day, the story had changed. *Roswell Daily Record* gathered more details or, according to the disbelievers, began to participate in a cover-up. On July 9, the *Record* reported on a recent press conference by Brigadier General Roger Ramey, commander of the Eighth Air Force at Fort Worth, Texas, who described the wreckage as a "bundle of tinfoil, broken wood beams, and rubber remnants of a balloon," all easily identifiable, mundane materials—and certainly not the makings of a spaceship. There were more details about the rancher, who was questioned for the story. He claimed to have discovered the wreckage on June 14, saying he and his son "came upon a large area of bright wreckage," which he described as being made of "rubber strips, tinfoil, rather tough paper and sticks." On the Fourth of July, he picked up some of the debris, and after hearing stories of UFOs on the next day, July 5, he decided he should contact the authorities. On July 7 he reached out to the sheriff of Roswell, who then notified Major Marcel.

---

[7]   The air force's official recount of the crash, known as The Roswell Report, acknowledges a high variance in estimated sightings, noting that some unnamed researchers had estimated "there were as many as 800 sightings during that period."

Here we encounter one of the biggest, most-often-ignored questions about the Roswell story: Would Brazel have bothered to report any of this if he hadn't heard reports of UFOs in other parts of the country?

Either way, Ramey's press conference and the rancher's actual statement put the matter to rest for most of the public until about 1978, when the *National Enquirer*[8] published a piece reporting that Marcel, now retired, claimed he had recovered UFO debris near Roswell back in 1947. The same year the *Enquirer* ran this story, a UFO researcher named Stanton Friedman met with Marcel to investigate his claims. Friedman's conversations would later launch much of the modern mythology surrounding Roswell today. Two years later, authors William L. Moore and Charles Berlitz published a book called *The Roswell Incident*, which they based on interviews with people who claimed to be present at Roswell in 1947, and have first- or secondhand knowledge of strange events that allegedly occurred at the same time. From there, the story grew legs of its own, and over time it diverged significantly from the original reports. This growth was massively accelerated by media of the 1980s and '90s, such as the TV show *Unsolved Mysteries*, which aired a dramatized re-creation of the event. As more and more TV shows and authors picked up the story, adding their own twists on the narrative, the overall thrust of the story changed—this was not really a weather balloon, it was implied—it was, instead, a cover-up of a craft from another world. The most common version of the story now, which has attained the status of folklore, argues that there were also bodies, or possibly living aliens, aboard the craft when it crashed. This is a rather crucial detail that simply does not exist in the initial reports, regardless of how the official story, and the speculative rumor mill, evolved over time.

The odd part about Roswell is that both skeptics and diehard UFO fans agree there was a cover-up. They just don't agree on what exactly was being covered up. The more skeptical tend to accept that the US Air Force actively

---

[8] The *National Enquirer* is a long-running, US-based tabloid known for immensely controversial reporting tactics, erroneous reports, and biases.

covered up Project Mogul and didn't take particular pains to dispel any speculation that distracted from this cover-up. Again, a lie within a lie within a lie. However, the changing official story and numerous perceived inconsistencies in accounts over time also give the true believers enough fodder to keep the story going. There's something quintessentially human about the quest to discover alien life—and something just as human in the tendency to cast aside facts if they contradict our preexisting views of reality.

For those who believe the cover-up hinges on genuine extraterrestrials, there's an immediate question: Who, exactly, orchestrated this grand conspiracy, and why? It certainly couldn't have been the entirety of the US government—there's no way the majority of full-time employees, whether civilian or military, could be aware of every classified project. So, if there was some top-secret conspiracy that wasn't Project Mogul, it would likely still have been helmed by a dedicated group with special access to a closely guarded cache of information. According to some conspiracy theorists, that group is real. They work in secret, and they exist entirely to address the massive threat posed by extraterrestrials. Their name? Majestic 12.

MAJESTIC 12

ANOTHER, LESS WELL-KNOWN piece of UFO conspiracy folklore hinges on the idea of a shadowy cabal, working in secret to manage government relationships with extraterrestrials. In this conspiracy theory, aliens are real, the government has had a long record of interaction with them, and for one reason or another, they absolutely do not want the public to know.

According to the story, in 1984, a documentary producer named Jaime Shandera received an anonymous envelope through his mail slot. The envelope had a New Mexico postmark and contained nothing other than a roll of undeveloped 35mm film. Shandera then took the film to his friend William

"Bill" Moore, a conspiracy researcher. Moore developed the film at his own home, and discovered it contained photos of eight pages of a classified document. This file, if legitimate, told a secret history of the events at Roswell.

THE MJ-12

Supposedly enumerated in the Eisenhower Briefing, the original "designated members" of the Majestic 12 (MJ-12) were thought to be:

Lloyd Berkner—physicist and engineer

Detlev Bronk—biophysicist

Vannevar Bush—engineer and inventor who headed the US Office of Scientific Research and Development during World War II

James Forrestal—secretary of defense

Gordon Gray—a long-time government official and lawyer deep in the world of defense and national security

Roscoe H. Hillenkoetter—CIA director who later became a governing board member of National Investigations Committee on Aerial Phenomena

Lieutenant Commander Jerome Clarke Hunsaker—US airman and aeronautics researcher

Donald H. Menzel—theoretical astronomer and astrophysicist

Lieutenant General Robert M. Montague

Rear Admiral Sidney Souers—another CIA director

General Nathan F. Twining—US Air Force

General Hoyt Vandenberg—US Air Force

While the US publicly dismissed most sightings, and was quick to launch investigations tracing those sightings to mundane causes, these photographs of pages argued there was a hidden strategy at play. The document, dated to 1952, appeared to be a briefing from the director of the CIA for President Eisenhower. It described several UFO incidents from

1947 into the 1950s, and claimed that then-President Truman, aware of an existential threat posed by extraterrestrials, secretly appointed a committee of twelve government officials to investigate. This group included members of the military and scientists, aiming to figure out not just how to respond to the Roswell crash but how to deal with other alien incursions that would doubtlessly occur in the future.[9] According to this account, the name Majestic 12 came from the group's size.

If true, this would be absolutely stunning news. Moore and Shandera originally chose to keep the film (and thus the document) secret, sharing them with a small number of like-minded UFO researchers, like Stanton Friedman. All three would later claim they received anonymous phone calls directing them to discover further documents, including the "Cutler/Twining" memo, which they also believed confirmed the existence of Majestic-12.[10] An anonymous source also appears to have contacted other authors in the UFO sphere, offering something like these documents. It seems that if Shandera and Moore wouldn't play ball, someone very much wanted this to enter the public conversation. As rumors about the documents spread through the small but growing ufology community, more and more people asked the three men for the evidence. Whether accidental or orchestrated, leaks began. Ultimately, in 1987, an author named Timothy Good took the info to the mainstream when he published aspects of the story in his book *Above Top Secret*. Later that year, he also spoke about MJ-12 at a UFO conference.

Not everyone was convinced. One author, Philip Klass, sent a copy of the materials directly to the FBI. The FBI soundly and categorically debunked

---

[9] This document has also become known as the "Eisenhower Briefing." In addition to describing the purpose of the group, the memo advised Eisenhower that its mission was important and must continue through the term of the new administration.

[10] The Cutler/Twining memo is a document supposedly found while Shandera, Moore, and Friedman were searching declassified files in the National Archives. According to the story, it is a memo from Robert Cutler, Eisenhower's assistant, to General Nathan F. Twining, and contains an explicit reference to MJ-12. Historians largely believe this to be a forgery, purposely planted to bolster the credibility of the original memo.

the document, dismissing it by literally scrawling the word "BOGUS" across the front page. Other investigators point out numerous signs of forgery, including the fact that Truman's signature appears to have been pasted on the page. There were also various discrepancies that would have easily been recognized by foreign intelligence agencies—irregular date notation, format, and so on.

Another bombshell dropped in 1989, but it wasn't the one ufologists were hoping for. Bill Moore, the second person to have seen the MJ-12 memo, attended a MUFON[11] conference where he announced that he had been actively involved in another conspiracy: helping the US government spread disinformation in the UFO community to distract ufologists from actual classified projects. He stated that he had been providing the government information about the UFO community in exchange for the material that later went into his books. He seemed to genuinely believe MJ-12 was a sort of reward for his work with the US Air Force's disinformation campaigns.

The news was not well received, and Moore soon left the UFO community in disgrace. It seems that Majestic-12 was, at heart, a conspiracy. It wasn't about extraterrestrials, but instead about disinformation, a propaganda move to disguise actual aviation research from foreign adversaries.[12] If this is the case—and evidence overwhelmingly indicates it is—then the conspiracy was successful. In fact, it was more successful than its original authors could have ever imagined. MJ-12 remains a hot topic of conversation in UFO forums, where it is often treated as an accepted fact. And in defense of the original ufologists beguiled by this operation, they themselves seemed to, with the exception of Bill Moore, genuinely believe the story was true. The story has been repeatedly debunked by now, so why does it continue to circulate in the UFO sphere?

---

[11] MUFON, short for the Mutual UFO Network, is a civilian, nonprofit group of volunteers studying reports of UFO sightings.

[12] For more on this strategy, see chapter 5 on propaganda.

The answer can be found, at least in part, in a version of what Emily Dickinson might have called a "slanted truth"—the MJ-12 forgery describes a fictional group, but one that functions very much like another kind of real, often-secretive organization: the think tank.

At the most basic level, a think tank is a pretty good idea. It's a research institute that provides context, expertise, investigation, and guidance on any number of topics. These groups can be a hybrid of private-public interests, and some function as semiautonomous agencies within the government. Others may be closely associated with a certain political party or private business. They're powered by private donations and grants and, like lobbyists, spend a great deal of time trying to move the needle of policy, up to and including drafting legislation. While something like the think tank existed in various countries far before World War II, these organizations experienced massive growth during the days of the Cold War—which was, conveniently, the time during which MJ-12 was allegedly formed. According to James McGann, writing for the Foreign Policy Research Institute, more than half of the world's current think tanks were established after 1980. Some of these organizations, known as "global policy institutes," advise world governments on any number of policies or goals, including things that may seem shadowy or unethical to outsiders.

Washington, DC, is home to somewhere around 400 different think tanks, each of which focuses on crafting policy and advising politicians. As of 2021, the top three most influential think tanks—the Belfer Center for Science and International Affairs, the Earth Institute, and the Heritage Foundation—all focus on any number of at-times contradictory goals, but none seem particularly concerned with the concept of extraterrestrials. Their triumphs and controversies are, at heart, all earthly concerns.

"Well," the true believers may say, "that just proves there *are* shadowy groups at play, and just because the MJ-12 story isn't true doesn't mean *something* like that isn't happening."

And here's where it gets crazy: if you're one of the people who think that, you're absolutely right.

UAP REPORT (2021)

WHILE PROJECT BLUE BOOK'S actual conclusions were disappointing for many ufologists, the more conspiratorially minded never quite gave up the ghost, and remained convinced the government continued tracking UFO reports, in secret. These concerns were confirmed when, in 2021, the government published a new report on UFOs, which they now refer to as unidentified aerial phenomena, or UAP. The report came in two versions: one, fairly short, for public consumption, and another, lengthier, classified version for Congress. The public report is titled *Preliminary Assessment: Unidentified Aerial Phenomena*. It's a nine-page analysis of phenomena previously considered rumor. It's the thing ufologists had dreamed of for decades: disclosure.

In 2017, the *New York Times* exposed the Pentagon's previously secret, mysterious UFO program known as Advanced Aerospace Threat Identification Program, or AATIP, which launched the previously unknown Luis Elizondo into the public eye. Elizondo is a former employee of the Office of the Under Secretary of Defense for Intelligence and Security (OUSD[I&S]) and a former US Army counterintelligence special agent. He headed AATIP. AATIP was a $22–29 million special access program initiated by the Defense Intelligence Agency in order to study UAPs. As with the earlier case of Project Blue Book, a contingent of the public still believes there's more to the story. And they may well be correct, as the substance of the second report remains classified. This program had been in operation since at least 2007. It was created by then-Senate Majority Leader Harry Reid with support from Senators Ted Stevens and Daniel Inouye. The formation of this group planted the seed that would later grow into this strange report.

The program, which operated until 2012, wasn't exactly classified, but it had zero publicity. The declassified report contains 144 total cases, 80 of which were detected on multiple sensors. It also lists 11 incidents where American warplanes had near midair collisions with unknown objects. Perhaps most importantly, in 18 of those 144 cases, the objects sighted appear to have exhibited unusual flight characteristics. Why is this important? It indicates the possibility of extant technology beyond the understanding of the US military. Until the military knows who created this, the nation is left in a frightening position. The assessment determines these sightings have more than one explanation and groups sightings into several broad categories: airborne clutter, natural atmospheric phenomena, governmental or industrial development programs, foreign adversary systems, and "other."

Airborne clutter is exactly what it sounds like: sky trash. The report describes the category thusly: "These objects include birds, balloons, recreational unmanned aerial vehicles (UAV), or airborne debris like plastic bags that muddle a scene and affect an operator's ability to identify true targets, such as enemy aircraft."

The next group, natural atmospheric phenomena, functions as a catch-all category for phenomena already understood by science, though in some cases these occurrences can be pretty rare, adding to their likelihood of being misidentified. It includes things like "ice crystals, moisture, and thermal fluctuations that may register on some infrared and radar systems."

The third category is a little juicier, with the report specifically stating, "Some UAP observations could be attributable to developments and classified programs by U.S. entities. We were unable to confirm, however, that these systems accounted for any of the UAP reports we collected." This means it's possible the program ran into one or more classified projects concerning tech the public doesn't know about—and if so, the groups running these projects were not forced to reveal their existence to investigators.

The next category is, perhaps, the most frightening for the authors: foreign adversary systems. "Some UAP," the report concludes, "may be technologies deployed by China, Russia, another nation, or a nongovernmental entity." Why is this so disturbing? Well, to put it bluntly, the US spends a massive amount of money and time trying to stay as up-to-date as possible on the capabilities of rival powers, and the smallest edge, no matter how expensive, can make a crucial difference on the battlefield. This process of gathering information is comprehensive and ongoing. It includes things like an asset calling US authorities to say, "Hey, so-and-so has invented a new ballistic missile." But it also includes things like monitoring a professor's work while tracing their recent travel, mapping out

The US spends a massive amount of money and time trying to stay as up-to-date as possible on the capabilities of rival powers.

their sphere of contacts, and when necessary, correlating that with reports of sensitive substances being imported by a foreign country.

From these various seemingly unrelated pieces of information, analysts can build out predictions and timelines, ranked in terms of both probability and concern. This means that, if a foreign, earthly enemy made something that remains inexplicable after repeated, direct observation, there would have been innumerable indicators of its research and construction leading up to those observations. So multiple agencies would have had to miss some pretty blatant signals over a fairly long period of time. And, if that's true, then we have NO IDEA what else that enemy power could be working on.

That category alone could be said to justify the cost of programs like these. It's important work, and ongoing. But for everyone who wants something a little more out of this world, you can't beat that final category: the tantalizing, vague, and perhaps ominous "other." It's the empty seat at the table of explanations, and the authors take monumental pains to never say words like "alien" or "extraterrestrial," as doing so would require a mountain of proof that—again, officially—does not exist. Even the mention of these and related terms would be seen as a massive blow to US credibility; to more cynical foreign observers, it would sound like cartoonishly clumsy propaganda. Here's how the writers of the report thread the needle:

> Although most of the UAP described in our dataset probably remain unidentified due to limited data or challenges to collection processing or analysis, we may require additional scientific knowledge to successfully collect on, analyze and characterize some of them. We would group such objects in this category pending scientific advances that allowed us to better understand them. UAPTF [Unidentified Aerial Phenomena Task Force] intends to focus additional analysis on the small number of cases where a UAP appeared to display unusual flight characteristics or signature management.

Let's unpack this. First, they're noting the small sample size available, and the lack of substantial data for a lot of the reports. Secondly, they're saying we literally may not be scientifically advanced enough to understand what we're seeing—and some of these things in the sky *do* appear to be intelligently operated. Then, there's this passage, one that astonished skeptics and ufologists alike:

> Some UAP appeared to remain stationary in winds aloft, move against the wind, maneuver abruptly, or move at considerable speed, without discernible means of propulsion. In a small number of cases, military aircraft systems processed radio frequency (RF) energy associated with UAP sightings.

The report concludes that some UAP are genuine physical objects—and they could be dangerous, posing "a hazard to safety of flight" and "a broader danger if some instances represent sophisticated collection against U.S. military activities by a foreign government or demonstrate a breakthrough aerospace technology by a potential adversary."

Toward the end, the authors seem to anticipate the public disappointment in both the brevity and the vagueness of the report. They request better reporting standards, more consolidation of data, and deeper analysis. Furthermore, they want aviators to experience less stigma reporting strange things in the sky. They also want these aviators not to halt tests or training, but to keep their eyes on whatever they're seeing for as long as possible, and report back. The conclusion notes the advantages of expanding data collection through algorithms, an undeniably smart move to identify a baseline for unusual stuff and to potentially identify hotspots or clusters. Being a government document, the report also explicitly calls for increased investment—like most government initiatives, they need more money. They propose three new initiatives—a UAP Collection Strategy, UAP R&D Technical Roadmap, and a UAP Program Plan—to help direct the investment. It may sound like a bit of a cash grab, but it isn't an unfair request. The proposed next steps will need a ton of coordination, new techniques, and so on. Each of those comes with a price tag.

So what happens now? It seems the figurative UFO is still up in the air in that regard. It isn't as if the sightings popped up during a discrete period of time and then stopped—this is an ongoing series of events. Public reaction will determine how the political class handles an investigation. If supporting further research feels like a ticket to reelection, most politicians will support it.

It's also reasonable to wonder what's in that classified report. There may be specifics that change the conversation, but it's tough to guess whether anything in there would be considered revelatory by the public. Most likely it contains other classified information about US sensor capabilities, surveillance methods, and possibly secret technology/development programs.

Yet in the fertile soil of secrecy, speculation thrives. In the US alone, around 65 percent of people believe alien life exists on other planets, and in 2019, reports of UFO sightings nearly doubled from the year before. Like our ancient ancestors, humans today remain enraptured by the mysteries of the sky above us and the tantalizing possibility—the statistical certitude—that somewhere out there is *proof*, proof that life on our little blue rock is not unique. That somewhere amid the sprawling, incomprehensible vastness of the universe, there is something, somehow, *like us*. That despite everything we know about the laws of physics, the sheer vastness of space, and the unstoppable passage of time, one day we or our descendants will be able to say, "We are not alone."

This urge is primal. Programs like AATIP are objective investigations, and forgeries like MJ-12 are fanciful fiction, but both serve to feed that fundamental urge for cosmic connection. And it seems millions of people, from children to astronauts, from USAF investigators to skeptics and hardcore ufologists alike still make time to gaze upward occasionally, and ask that single, beautiful question so common to us all:

"What if?"

CHAPTER FIVE

PROPAGANDA

THE CONSCIOUS AND INTELLIGENT MANIPULATION OF THE ORGANIZED HABITS AND OPINIONS of the masses is an important element in democratic society. Those who manipulate this unseen mechanism of society constitute an invisible government which is the true ruling power of our country. We are governed, our minds are molded, our tastes formed, and our ideas suggested, largely by men we have never heard of.... It is they who pull the wires that control the public mind.

—*Propaganda*, Edward Bernays, 1928

You've seen propaganda before. When it's working correctly, you haven't noticed. A politician describes, in detail, a fictional scenario about how terrible life will be for America's children if a new immigration bill passes. Through lurid anecdotes, with no supporting evidence, and harrowing, visceral descriptions of starving children in breadlines, the politician transports their audience to a world that doesn't yet exist—but *certainly will*, they imply, if you don't join the cause and vote the way you should.

A celebrity attributes their clear skin (and therefore, it's implied, their successful career) to Brand X eye cream. An athlete, fresh off a record-breaking streak of wins, announces their own custom brand of sneaker. Later, they mention you should also drink more Gatorade.

You may not have children. If you live in the United States today, odds are your ancestors were immigrants. Still, that politician's unfounded tall tale may have captured some part of your mind.

You may have nothing in common with that A-list actor other than seeing their films, but you may also feel increasingly concerned about those wrinkles deepening around your eyes as you age.

And while you know a magic shoe or sports drink cannot, in fact, make you "Be Like Mike," this message speaks to a deeper, less-conscious part of your brain. Soon enough you decide to "Just Do It." You buy your first pair of Air Jordans.

You buy Brand X eye cream.

You vote for or against some mythical story.

In each case your decisions feel self-determined. You are the author of their real-world consequences.

This is propaganda.

It's ubiquitous. It's clever. It's insidious. You are under its influence as you read this book.

Propaganda is the antecedent of modern advertising. Modern propaganda was born when those in power realized that the curation of information can be much more effective than censoring it. Shoes, eye cream, political positions, wars. The subject is almost beside the point—it's not *what* you say, in short, but *how* you say it.

Many people incorrectly assume propaganda is a recent phenomenon, but the word itself dates back to the seventeenth century. And evidence of the basic concept behind it—crafting a message, often deceptively, to guide a large group of individuals toward a single set of attitudes or opinions—dates back into antiquity. Propaganda predates the printing press, the radio, the newspaper, and social media. It is platform agnostic. It thrives on modern communication platforms as easily as it did in the theaters of ancient Greece. It was a fundamental piece of all great conquerors' strategies, from David and Alexander to Mansa Musa, Genghis Khan, and George Washington. Propaganda was a fundamental piece of the conflicts in the Middle Ages, as well as the later American independence movement. Whenever and wherever society has a sense of common interests, you can find examples of something like propaganda.

> **Many people incorrectly assume propaganda is a recent phenomenon. The word, however, dates back to the seventeenth century.**

While propaganda is not always inaccurate, it is often misleading. Consider: a public health campaign raising awareness of diabetes could be defined as propaganda, as could a heartbreaking advertisement about the importance of adopting neglected dogs from animal shelters. Yet slanderous anti-Semitic pamphlets, all too frequently published throughout history, are also propaganda.

THANK GOD FOR PROPAGANDA

As a term, propaganda traces its origins to 1622 and the formation of the *Sacra Congregatio de Propaganda Fide* (the Sacred Congregation for the Propagation of the Faith) by Pope Gregory XV. Having just emerged from the teeth of the Reformation in the 16th century, only to walk right into the religiously motivated Thirty Years' War beginning in 1618, the Catholic Church was concerned about the Protestant-Catholic balance of power not just in Europe (which would effectively be settled in 1648 by the Treaty of Westphalia) but in Asia, Africa, and the Americas, where European powers had been "exploring" for two hundred years. The purpose of "The Propaganda," as it was referred to colloquially, was to coordinate the Church's missionary activity around the world. Or put another way, to establish and maintain centralized control of how missionaries convinced people to become Catholic. In service of those efforts, The Propaganda ran a seminary for training missionaries and operated a printing press that produced things like hymn books and the Catechism in many languages. The group exists to this day, with an almost identical mission, but under a different name: The Congregation for the Evangelization of Peoples. A name it adopted in 1967 under Pope Paul VI, in a curious if not convenient bit of timing when one considers that 1967 was a volatile year that seemed to find the entire world papered over with . . . you guessed it, propaganda.

In the above examples, we see commonalities—and one crucial distinction. All three examples have a clear angle, a bias. They're meant to *persuade*. "Sure," one could argue, "but that's not different from advertising, is it?" We'll get to advertising in a moment, but first we must acknowledge the primary difference—the thing that can make propaganda so dangerous. Two of the campaigns, diabetes awareness and the importance of adopting pets, happen to be based in fact. The third example, racist vitriol straight out of hoaxes such as *The Protocols of the Elders of Zion*,[1] dresses up age-old prejudice and fiction, costuming it as fact and hoping the average reader isn't sharp enough to recognize the grift. In worst-case scenarios, successful propaganda campaigns can beguile the unaware audience, tricking them into supporting very real, dangerous things. Propaganda can be based in fact, and it can be based in fiction. It's often based on some convenient, cynical mix of both. In the world of propaganda, the truth matters only if it supports the end goal: convincing you of a certain idea. And it does this not by appealing to intellect but to emotion, through the use of catchy slogans, powerful images, and above all, the control of which facts or lies are allowed to enter a given conversation.

For this reason, propaganda is best described as *weaponized information*. While it's true that not all propaganda is inherently "bad," many propaganda campaigns are made in bad faith, a cynical, ruthless push to make you think a certain way about a certain thing, facts be damned. Once we recognize the common approaches, we cannot unsee the tactics applied—a loose collection of high rhetoric, oddly similar to information wars waged by the empires of old.

The emotional appeal. In the earlier example, our politician either didn't need facts and statistics, or found the truth was at odds with their goal. So instead of examining the mountains of context and data involved in any question about immigration policy, they decided to tell a spooky campfire story implying that disagreeing with them was tantamount to not caring about the future of America's children. The emotional appeal exists as an inherent threat—what will happen to the children, the future?

Second, *the testimonial.* Our athlete and our celebrity are good at two things: sports and celebrity. Their success in these fields lends a sort of "perceived credibility" passport, meaning that while neither of these individuals

---

[1] First published in Russia in 1903, *The Protocols of the Elders of Zion* is a work of fiction purporting to reveal a grand conspiracy among the world's Jewish population to control the planet. Despite being repeatedly and thoroughly debunked (it was originally based in racist political satire), it remains popular in neo-Nazi circles in the modern day.

is, say, a podiatrist or a dermatologist, some members of the public give these celebrities' opinions more weight than they would the scientific conclusions of actual dermatologists and podiatrists. This is also an example of a third technique: the *transference*, a cognitive bait and switch.

"I like this actor," thinks someone watching that eye cream commercial. "I remember how funny they were in that comedy last year." This audience member's positive perception of this celebrity transfers to other things the celebrity appears to have positive feelings for.

There are other propagandistic techniques, all aiming to curate your opinion in ways you may not fully comprehend. Through techniques like bandwagoning, name-calling, and the old "just plain folks like you and me" tactic,[2] the adept propagandist can subtly push people toward supporting any number of opinions and beliefs, even if those opinions and mandates are self-harming.

If modern propaganda has a patriarch, it is Edward Louis Bernays. Born in 1891, Bernays, who was the nephew of Sigmund Freud, began to unravel the power of propaganda in the early 1900s. He stumbled across the idea while working for two obscure medical journals in 1913: *The Dietetic and Hygienic Gazette* and *The Medical Review of Reviews*.[3] It's important to note Bernays was not an idealist at this point. He wanted only to increase the circulation and profit of these publications. He'd recently tried a few out-of-the-box solutions, such as pushing the owner to publish catchier, more controversial opinions and distributing free copies of the *Medical Review* to most of the 137,000 physicians licensed to practice in the United States at that time. Yet these innovations didn't seem to make much of a difference.

---

[2] Politicians are incredibly fond of the "plain folks" tactic, which is why you'll see so many political ads with a candidate inexplicably chopping wood, driving a pickup, or for some reason, mending a fence on a fictional farm. The trick here is that, by appearing to be one of the "common" people, they can remove their association with Washington, DC, and trick the audience into thinking "this person is just like me, so I must agree with their ideas, which also must be common sense."

[3] While the title may sound a tad absurd, peer review remains a vital, often-overlooked step in any serious scientific research.

He needed something bigger, something unexpected, some way to transform the obstacle of obscurity into an opportunity for success. He found this opportunity in a letter written to the journal, a doctor's rave review of a play called *Damaged Goods*. Written by French playwright Eugène Brieux, this story explores the life of a man with syphilis as he marries and eventually has a child afflicted with the same condition.

Ordinarily no journal would consider publishing a favorable review of such a divisive, sexually frank piece. Public discussion of sexually transmitted disease was taboo; it flew in the face of all contemporary moral conventions, as did any mention of remedies for those conditions. Edward saw his opportunity. Bernays convinced the journal's owner to publish the review—and he also convinced an A-list actor of the day, Richard Bennett, to star in a production of the show. At first, things looked dire. He and the journal's owner couldn't get financial support for the play. It was simply too sordid for well-to-do members of society to consider being associated with it. So, Bernays began thinking about the problem from a different angle. People may be gun-shy about supporting something controversial—in this case, a play about STDs—but how would they respond to supporting a *cause*?

To this end, Bernays formed a new organization associated with the *Medical Review*. He presented this group, which he called the Sociological Fund Committee, as an organization dedicated to public health education, the arts, and the good of humanity overall. He requested that each prospective member of the committee join by contributing four dollars,[4] which, in addition to membership, granted them one ticket to the show.

Shortly after forming, the committee attracted the attention of hundreds of people—including Rockefellers, Roosevelts, and Vanderbilts; locally known religious figures; and businessmen such as Dr. William J. Schieffelin, another old-money scion whose company had recently introduced a new treatment for syphilis in the US. Edward asked some of the

---

[4] Four dollars in 1913 was the equivalent of a little more than $110 today. Remember, Bernays was aiming for the well-off members of society, the people who could steer larger conversations.

more prominent committee members to publicly endorse the organization and the play itself. It was a favor they readily, and unanimously, granted.

Damaged Goods, a play that once would have never seen the light of an American stage, became a runaway success. Reviews published in March 1913 characterized the play as a symbol of a turning point in American cultural discourse. Edward recognized the immense (if deceptive) value of having the support of important people, and soon he imagined replicating this process to bring more injustices to the public eye—combating drug use, for instance, or human trafficking.

That same year, Edward traveled to Europe. He made the trip to learn exactly what had happened with *Damaged Goods*. What motivated a mass of influential people to move in concert toward the goal he set? Could this phenomenon be replicated again? And if so, how? He could think of no one better to ask than his uncle, Sigmund Freud.

The specifics of their conversations are lost to history, but Bernays returned a changed man. He began to repeat the steps he'd established with *Damaged Goods*, linking entertainment to larger, ostensibly humanitarian goals. *Causes.* He moved into consumer goods and began working for the US Committee on Public Information, where he popularized war bonds and disseminated propaganda to aid in the war effort.

Bernays went on to tie Lucky Strike cigarettes to the women's suffrage movement, which propelled smoking to new heights once those cigarettes became known as "torches of freedom." The Aluminum Company of America hired him to convince the public of the benefits of water fluoridation. While working on President Calvin Coolidge's 1924 reelection campaign, he invented the concept of the pancake breakfast. Bernays did quite a lot for the concept of North American breakfast, in fact. (Though perhaps not a lot for people's health.) In another public relations coup, he became the reason Americans eat bacon in the morning. It's a story that sounds almost too fanciful to be true, and it bears further examination.

Before the Age of Bernays, the vast majority of post-industrial-era Americans ate a light breakfast—coffee and bread, or some juice, perhaps, or the newly popular processed cereal. This was a marked change from the pre-industrial, more agrarian days, when people living on farms typically ate a heavier morning meal to sustain them through the demanding physical labor of the coming day. People were increasingly moving from farms to cities, and this change in location led to a change in lifestyle. The Roaring Twenties created a growing consumer society. People tended toward lighter, faster meals in the morning. Diet fads of the time argued for more vegetarian diets in general, and rumor had it that an overly heavy breakfast could cause indigestion, leading to poor performance at work. Additionally, people living in cities weren't doing the same intensive labor as earlier generations out on farms, and life in the city meant most people didn't have the space to raise their own chickens or pigs. These factors combined to make the hearty, heavy bacon-and-eggs breakfast of farmers a thing of the past. The Beech-Nut Packing Company, perhaps best known for baby food, had a problem with this trend. Beech-Nut made a number of consumer goods, but it was also in the pork game at the time—and the company needed to sell more. Specifically, they needed a way to unload all their bacon, despite the public's growing disinterest. Since traditional advertising didn't seem to reverse this trend, they contacted Bernays—and he had a plan.

First, he decided to narrow Beech-Nut's focus. Selling bacon in general was too broad, in his opinion. It had to be associated both with a specific meal and, as always, a cause. The meal, he decided, would be breakfast. A hearty breakfast featuring bacon would evoke America's rural heartland. It was nostalgic, reminding consumers, perhaps, of the halcyon "good old days" on some mythical family farm. While people might not all live on farms, he reasoned, they would likely have some fond associations with the idea. The cause, he concluded, would be one near and dear to every American of the day: their own health. He knew a typical advertisement from the company making the bacon might not hold much weight with the public, so he asked himself who would be best to champion this claim of bacon's health benefits. Eventually the answer became obvious. John and Jane Q. Public might not trust a pork company's claims about bacon, but they *would* trust a doctor. Especially, he reasoned, if multiple doctors appeared to agree on the same point.

And so Bernays went to speak with the doctor he'd retained at his PR agency. His first question was simple, something like, "Do you think a heavier breakfast might be more beneficial than a lighter one?" The doctor—again, to be clear, an employee of the firm—readily agreed.[5] Bernays then asked this employee, who was later described as "a famous New York doctor," to write to 5,000 of his colleagues, asking them, in a very carefully phrased way, whether they agreed with this idea. According to Bernays, 4,500 doctors responded, agreeing that a heavier breakfast was indeed better for you than a lighter breakfast. From these responses, Bernays created a "study"—the early example of the "four out of five doctors recommend"[6] approach so common today—and had it published in newspapers and magazines across the country. He also made sure these newspapers mentioned bacon and eggs as an integral part of any "healthy" breakfast.

And it worked. People weren't buying bacon because it was tasty. It instead became a matter of following expert advice. After all, these were doctors, not slick ad executives. Beech-Nut's profits soared, and as of 2020, the average person living in the US eats around eighteen pounds of bacon per year.

While this fundamental shift in dietary habits may have indirectly led to some untimely deaths, it paled in comparison to another of Bernays's machinations. Decades later, when the massively wealthy United Fruit Company sought to overthrow the elected leader of Guatemala in the early 1950s, Bernays was instrumental in the campaign for the hearts and minds of Americans. Through various fronts, he barraged Congress and the American public with misinformation and propaganda, convincing the nation that overthrowing a foreign government is a humanitarian act.

Today, Edward Bernays is lauded as the father of public relations, and his methods are still in use. His legacy is complicated, and crucial

---

[5] It's important to note that, while Bernays claimed the agency's employee was being objective, the fact that this doctor occupied a paid position makes it a little tougher to take his claim at face value.

[6] According to Bernays, the headlines were something like "4,500 Physicians Urge a Heavy Breakfast in Order to Improve the Health of the American People."

to understanding the modern information war surrounding the concept of the "post-truth" world. During his time, he wrote extensively about his practices, philosophies, and accomplishments, most notably in his seminal work, *Propaganda*, which is freely available online and should be required reading for any student of mass communication.

We witness these techniques on a continual basis, often under different names. When they're meant to sell us cars or fast food, we call them ads. When they're meant to sell us wars, we call them propaganda. And, most recently, in the realm of journalism, we call this phenomenon "fake news."

FAKE NEWS

ACCORDING TO INVESTIGATIVE JOURNALIST Sharyl Attkisson, the modern meaning of "fake news" was popularized by a left-wing website called First Draft News, which was established in 2015 to correct the false, misleading, or erroneous reports disseminated by conservative sources proliferating on social media platforms. Though the website was originally founded as a news watchdog, its lasting legacy has been coining a phrase former US president Donald Trump has wielded as a thought-terminating cliché[7] used to dismiss or discredit any piece of reporting he personally disagreed with.

As with virtually all forms of propaganda, the use of "fake news" is an old technique. In the age of the Spanish Armada, for instance, both the Spanish and English monarchies deployed fake reports of sea battles and

---

[7] A thought-terminating cliché, also known as a "thought-stopper," is a common phrase that can be used to dismiss dissent or justify fallacious logic. In the modern day, calling something a "conspiracy theory" turns the phrase into one of these clichés—simply hearing it applied to a given concept or claim can make that claim appear less credible, regardless of whatever merits it may otherwise possess. Other examples of thought-terminating clichés include phrases such as "it is what it is," "whatever will be, will be," or "rules are rules."

other conflicts, spinning the narrative in ways they felt would be most advantageous to their goals. The only real difference between what we call fake news today and the propaganda of ages past is the medium of communication. For the first time in human history, we live in an era of constant, nearly instantaneous communication, in which we are besieged by an endless deluge of news, knowledge, purported facts, and claims from across the planet. The democratization of information and the ease of broadcasting one's thoughts to mass audiences has allowed everyone to become a performer, reporter, and publisher. This presents clear benefits, and clear dangers. Today, it's easier than ever to call someone in Chile all the way from Sweden, and speak in real time. Never before has it been so easy to acquire information. You can, for example, have a conversation about the periodic table or a pop song from the 1960s, then pull out your phone instantly to learn more details. Current estimates reckon the human species is generating about 1.145 trillion megabytes of data per day, every day—and the number will only rise going forward. Additionally, a single person—not necessarily a professional broadcaster, professor, or public figure—can instantly broadcast to millions over social media platforms.

It is impossible to overstate the significance of these technological changes. Like the discovery of fire, the invention of constant communication poses as much danger as it does opportunity. While the amount of information available has skyrocketed, the constraints of the human brain have remained unchanged. Our minds have evolved to recognize patterns and already relied heavily on cognitive shortcuts to navigate the natural, pre-electronic world. Now the poor human cerebrum—identical to that of our human ancestors living tens of thousands of years ago—is like a sailor in a hurricane, drowning in a chaotic torrent of advertisements, proposals, declarations, and propaganda. Today we spend about a third of our lifespan digesting knowledge. If you stayed awake for the rest of your life, without eating, without being distracted, and you lived for a thousand years, you as an individual would still never finish reading everything available online. Reading the entirety of Wikipedia alone would take about twenty years, if you somehow spent those two decades doing nothing but reading.

This means there is less and less time for considered thought, for synthesis and analysis of a piece of information. We increasingly tend to think in terms of headlines and broad strokes, and we are psychologically primed, physiologically hardwired, to prioritize the perceived credibility of headlines that reinforce our existing opinions.

This is a tremendous boon to propagandists. They are well aware of our cognitive limitations and devise strategies to target them. One common method is to create a fake website imitating a legitimate news source. One such scam was discovered in 2015, when a fraudster mimicked a Bloomberg.com story using the deceptive domain name "'Bloomberg.ma." Now defunct, the story on Bloomberg.ma successfully convinced some of its readers that Twitter had received a takeover offer to the tune of $31 billion, temporarily causing the company's stock price to jump by 8 percent. This approach, creating the appearance of credibility, is both widespread and menacing. In the US, far-right groups and foreign entities routinely create legitimate-sounding sources as platforms for the dissemination of disinformation[8] and propaganda. Ideological propaganda has also enjoyed a resurgence on social media, as algorithms work continuously to feed users content they are likely to agree with. While this is great for the bottom line of a business—it helps ensure a steady cycle of engagement, attention, and clicks—the practice can be

If you stayed awake for the rest of your life, without eating, without being distracted, and you lived for a thousand years, you as an individual would still never finish reading everything available online.

---

[8] While misinformation and disinformation both describe the spread of false claims, disinformation is the purposeful act of doing so. To wit, an old colleague sharing an antivaccination post on Facebook may be spreading misinformation, but a Russian-backed outlet manufacturing and propagating these claims to destabilize the West is spreading disinformation.

121

dangerous for the individual users, as they are less and less likely to see objective sources of information.

The power of propaganda goes further. As the twentieth century produced methods of communication that were faster and reached more people, governments, activist groups, corporations, and other institutions realized they could leverage the power of public perception toward any number of goals. And for governments, propaganda could do more than sway voters' opinions on a certain law or politician. In the US, Bernays's work leading to the coup in Guatemala set a precedent fundamentally altering the course of governmental public policy, creating a pattern that arguably continues in the modern day. Propaganda, the government found, could help you start wars.

MANUFACTURING WAR

FROM THE DAWN OF HUMANITY until the days of rival newspapers, the beliefs of communities have often been influenced by a relatively small number of authoritative voices such as spiritual leaders, for example, or members of an aristocracy. Various fringe theorists claim these influencers have, at one time or another, created the news rather than reporting it. It's unfortunately not an implausible claim. In fact, there's a compelling argument to be made that factions of the US government took the ideas of Bernays and ran with them, applying his techniques to other endeavors. For better or worse, the United States was less concerned with bacon, and more concerned with war.

When it comes to conflict, democratic countries have a complication that doesn't always exist in other governments: political leaders depend on elections to stay in office, and to win these elections they must have public support for their policies, up to and including international conflict. If a *casus belli* cannot be found, it can be manufactured. This leads us to what's commonly known as a "false flag" attack. In the US, the most famous example of a false flag is the infamous Gulf of Tonkin incident of 1964, which led to full US involvement in the Vietnam War.[9]

THE GULF OF TONKIN

THE STORY OF THE GULF OF TONKIN officially begins in Vietnam, but its roots date back much, much further, to the long-standing distrust the US held for the Soviet Union and communism in general since the Russian Revolution of 1917. Following the ideological declarations of the Truman Doctrine, the United States of the 1950s doubled down on this enmity, convinced that the Soviet Union and Communist China posed an ideological, existential threat to the American way of life.[10] Truman introduced the concept of domino theory—that the fall of one democratic country to communism could lead to increased instability in other countries in a given region, or across the world. This concern would carry on well past Truman's administration. In 1954, then-President Dwight D. Eisenhower stated the fall of French Indochina would result in a cascade of communist revolutions throughout the region. This concept held great influence over US policy after the Eisenhower administration as well. With Soviet expansion into Eastern Europe and the establishment of communist regimes in China, North Korea, and Cuba, fears of communist expansion across the globe grew as the years went on, accelerating during conflicts like the

---

[9]   A "casus belli" is an event or action that is used to justify a war or other conflict.

[10] The Truman Doctrine, issued by President Harry Truman in a speech to Congress in 1947, called for the United States to provide assistance to all democratic countries under threat by external or internal authoritarian (communist) forces. This assistance could include political and economic support, as well as possible military intervention.

123

Korean War and the Cuban missile crisis. By 1964, Americans were primed for conflict in Indochina. Here is the story Americans were told in the news coverage at the time.

Two US Navy destroyers, the USS *Maddox* and the USS *Turner Joy*, were stationed in a region called the Gulf of Tonkin, nowadays known as the East Vietnam Sea. Their position was strategic—these waters separate Vietnam from the Chinese island of Hainan. The ships were part of an effort to support military raids by South Vietnamese forces on the North Vietnamese coastal territory. On August 2, 1964, North Vietnamese forces launched an attack on the *Maddox*. On August 4, a second attack occurred. This time, the North Vietnamese targeted the *Turner Joy*. This second attack caused Congress to pass a resolution authorizing the federal government to "take all necessary measures" to protect US forces in Vietnam.

Nearly four decades later, the public would learn this story was not entirely true. Documents released by the National Security Agency in 2000 showed the second attack on August 4, the one used to justify a steep escalation in US military involvement in Vietnam, *never actually happened.* Officials had purposely misled the public, and in the time leading up to this grand deception, they had been actively ratcheting up tension along the coast, assisting the South Vietnamese forces in raids and strikes on islands controlled by the North Vietnamese. The attack on the *Maddox* did occur, though the ship suffered at best minimal damage, successfully avoiding the torpedoes and sailing away. In fact, it resumed its normal patrol the very next day, this time with the *Turner Joy* along for the ride. The two destroyers were miles away from the coast. And here the stories diverge.

The captain of the *Maddox*, John Herrick, had directed the ships to sail more than 100 miles away from the North Vietnamese-controlled coast. The ship reported multiple vessels appearing on sonar, and it looked as if they were coming from different directions, disappearing and reappearing in different locations. Herrick sent out a message, moving the ships as best he could. Pilots flying from the USS *Ticonderoga*, a nearby aircraft carrier, realized something was off about the situation. *Ticonderoga* Commander James Stockdale claimed the destroyers were just shooting at "phantom targets." He saw nothing on the sea. Was something wrong with the sonar? Around the same time, Captain Herrick concluded there might be something wrong with the sonar on his ship, or his rookie sonar operators might be struggling to interpret information. During the entirety of this incident, the *Turner Joy* detected zero enemy torpedoes, and today it's widely believed the *Maddox* sonar may have just been detecting the tops of waves.

On August 5, just a few hours later, Captain Herrick sent the following message: "Review of action makes many reported contacts and torpedoes fired appear doubtful. Freak weather effects on radar and overeager sonar operators may have accounted for many reports. No actual visual sighting by Maddox. Suggest complete evaluation before any further action taken."[11]

Despite Herrick's good-faith efforts to correct the events, Washington wanted a war—and finally had a justification for it. As long as the American public was left in the dark, there would be widespread support for military intervention in retaliation for what was being framed as an "unprovoked attack." Almost immediately, then-President Lyndon Johnson hit the airwaves, announcing:

> As President and Commander in Chief, it is my duty to the American people to report that renewed hostile actions against United States ships on the high seas in the Gulf of Tonkin have today required me to order the military forces of the United States to take action in reply. The initial attack on the destroyer Maddox, on August 2, was repeated today by a number of hostile vessels attacking two U.S. destroyers with torpedoes.[12]

Commander Stockdale was ordered to lead a strike of eighteen aircraft on the North Vietnamese, attacking an oil-storage facility inland, close to the site of the alleged incident. In later statements, Stockdale would say that with these attacks, the US launched a war under false pretenses. Two

---

[11] As related by Lieutenant Commander Pat Paterson, US Navy, in "The Truth About Tonkin" for *Naval History Magazine*, Volume 22, Number 1, February 2008.

[12] From Johnson's public speech to the American Public on August 4, 1964.

days after the strike, on August 7, Congress approved the Gulf of Tonkin Resolution, leading to a horrifying, tragic conflict that haunts Vietnam and the United States to the present day.

Not everyone believed the US government's story at the time, and the skeptics weren't just isolationists, hippies, and revolutionaries. Some military officials were convinced there was a conspiracy at play. As early as 1967, a former naval officer named John White stated that he believed "that President Johnson, Secretary [Robert] McNamara and the Joint Chiefs of Staff gave false information to Congress in their report about U.S. destroyers being attacked in the Gulf of Tonkin."

Over the years, these criticisms were swept under the rug. But slowly, a more accurate picture of what happened emerged. Decades after the war, investigations by experts like NSA historian Robert J. Hanyok appear to confirm White's, Stockdale's, and Herrick's accounts. Hanyok was able to verify the August 2 incident but found no evidence at all that any attack occurred on August 4. It gets worse. Hanyok also found the evidence had been cherry-picked to support going to war. Some of the signals allegedly detected on August 2 and 4 were falsified entirely, and others altered to reflect a different timeline.

Those purposely distorted reports were crucial evidence in the president's argument for war, and they were prioritized above the other reports, the majority of which concluded there was no attack on August 4. Does this mean that the Vietnam War would not have occurred if the American public had immediately known the truth about what happened? Not necessarily. Historical records indicate the Johnson administration was more than ready to increase its involvement in the conflict and had been steadily escalating its activities since well before those two days in August. Still, when something that looked like the right opportunity came along, the White House did not hesitate to pounce on it, and the war began, based largely on a lie. It's an uncomfortable truth, one widely acknowledged in the modern day—but it may not be the only example of manufacturing war.

In fact, as time would reveal, leaders in the United States not only used these tactics but were vulnerable to them.

HILL & KNOWLTON VERSUS IRAQ: THE DANGERS OF ASTROTURF

IN THE EARLY HOURS OF AUGUST 2, 1990, Iraqi president Saddam Hussein launched an invasion of neighboring Kuwait. Earlier that year, his government had publicly accused Kuwait of stealing petroleum. Some observers believe the decision to invade was made months beforehand, and that the stated cause of petroleum theft was only one of a number of reasons for the conflict.[13] The tiny, oil-rich nation was overtaken in a matter of days, and US leadership, despite having been supporters of Hussein during the Iran-Iraq War, threw its support behind the new Kuwaiti resistance movement. The US decision to defend Kuwait was widely supported. All major world powers condemned the invasion, including traditional allies of Iraq like France and India. In her defense of the anti-Iraq coalition's decision to confront Hussein, British Prime Minister Margaret Thatcher raised the specter of the 1930s, warning allies that appeasement would lead only to Hussein attempting to conquer the entirety of the Persian Gulf.

This wasn't the only rhetorical strategy employed to support war. In September 1990, Kuwait's UN representative Mohammad A. Abulhasan wrote an open letter accusing Iraqi forces of stealing massive amount of Kuwaiti assets, including vital medical equipment like dialysis machines and incubators. This vision of stolen incubators and the threat it represented to children became an international point of outrage in the lead-up to the conflict. The next month, the US Congressional Human Rights Caucus heard testimony from a fifteen-year-old Kuwaiti girl identified only by her

---

[13] Speculation about the "real" reason for the invasion usually hinges on the idea that Iraq was unable to pay off a $14 billion debt to Kuwait, which it had used to fund the Iran-Iraq War of the 1980s. Additionally, Iraq accused Kuwait of economic warfare due to disagreements over OPEC petroleum quotas.

first name, Nayirah. In this testimony, Nayirah stated she had personally witnessed Iraqi soldiers not just stealing incubators but taking babies out of them and leaving those children to die.

This testimony set the world and public opinion ablaze. It was cited multiple times by US senators, representatives, and then-President George H. W. Bush as a rationale for becoming involved in the conflict. To Americans, intervention was portrayed as a moral obligation. And it's easy to understand the emotional power of this idea: no one in their right mind would think of themselves as someone in support of cruelty to children. It made a clear case of good versus evil, simplifying a conflict into basic, human terms. Very soon after, the US led an international coalition to drive Iraq out of Kuwait, and entered the Gulf War.

Today we know that this testimony was false, manufactured by a group called Citizens for a Free Kuwait. As the possibility of war loomed on the horizon, the government of Kuwait created this fake grassroots organization, a ploy known as "astroturfing." With Citizens for a Free Kuwait as its front, the Kuwaiti government hired Hill & Knowlton, a PR firm largely invisible to the public but often instrumental—like, Bernays-level instrumental—in various international conflicts. Initially, Nayirah's story was amplified by Amnesty International, though they issued a correction when the falsehoods were exposed. Later investigations from multiple sources found that while Iraqi forces were indeed committing human-rights violations, the incubator story as depicted in Nayirah's testimony was at best wildly distorted. In fact, "Nayirah" was actually Nayirah Al-Sabah, the daughter of the Kuwaiti ambassador to the US.

In 1992, Kroll Associates released a report based on 250 interviews over a nine-week period, concluding the alleged crimes were, at the very least, enormously embellished if not outright fabricated. Nayirah herself noted she had seen only one child outside an incubator for a moment and, contrary to her testimony, had stopped by the hospital only for a few minutes rather than being a volunteer. Further, she said her statement had been prepared with assistance from Hill & Knowlton, leading to speculation that the firm may have written the statement itself and coached her on how best to deliver it.

Here's what actually happened. After being hired by Citizens for a Free Kuwait, Hill & Knowlton financed an extensive study to determine the best way to push the US leadership and public into armed conflict against Iraq. The study, a series of focus groups conducted by the Wirthington Group, concluded that emphasizing atrocities, especially the incubator story, proved to be the most effective strategy for galvanizing public opinion. Hill & Knowlton also had men on the inside. Two congressmen, Tom Lantos and John Porter, headed a nongovernmental organization called the Congressional Human Rights Foundation. It rented space in Hill & Knowlton's DC headquarters. To critics, this connection proved that Lantos and Porter were working off the books with Hill & Knowlton to advance their cause in the halls of Congress. While, officially, all parties involved deny purposely misleading the public, it remains a milestone in the application of propagandistic techniques. Through the power of PR, a foreign government was able to steer the ship of American policy abroad.

And while many questions surround the evolution of this campaign, one thing's for sure: Kuwait was far from the only foreign country attempting to guide the opinion of the US. Thanks to the rise of social media and online communication, you don't even have to send operatives in person nowadays; so much can be done online.

ONLINE PROPAGANDA WARS

IN THE AGE OF SOCIAL MEDIA, "authoritative" opinions are easy to generate and disseminate. It can be hard to evaluate their credibility, and therefore they can exert tremendous influence. Shills are paid to present a certain viewpoint as though it is their sincere, organic opinion, despite often using a set of talking points verbatim from a central source. Bots are programmed to swarm accounts or stories to amplify false claims or tear down valid ones. Translation can be another source of confusion or misdirection—an idiom or turn of phrase may not translate well, or a translator may purposely skew the tone of a statement to make it sound more warlike. Translation sources can often be obtuse about the choices they make, and purposeful mistranslations can be difficult to spot.

These efforts at disinformation aren't just the product of individuals or isolated groups of malcontents, fanatics, or trolls. Many are organized and sophisticated state-level operations designed to alter the course of international conversation. The world isn't just fighting wars on the ground—it's also now fighting them in the cloud. This is known as strategic information warfare. It's a type of asymmetric warfare, a phrase used to describe tactics that countries, individuals, and terrorist groups use to attack a conventionally superior opponent while avoiding direct confrontation. In the real, nondigital world, these strategies are adopted when the military abilities of two forces aren't just unequal; they're so fundamentally different that they cannot make the same sorts of attacks on each other. Examples of asymmetric warfare include things such as hijackings, suicide bombings, and guerilla tactics, allowing outnumbered forces to bedevil a conventionally stronger military. In short, why break the national budget trying to build your own aircraft carrier when you can, with much less cash and much less effort, build missiles capable of destroying enemy carriers, rendering their massive, expensive advantage useless?

Asymmetric tactics are as old as the most ancient of empires and continue to be employed today, due both to necessity and efficacy. They put the defending force on its heels. After all, the attacker has time on their side. They can extensively prepare for a specific attack, and have the ability to choose when and where it happens. In contrast, defending forces must prepare for all possible potential attacks and constantly guard against them. This is expensive, labor intensive, and never 100 percent effective. Information warfare is also an old practice—consider the stories of Voice of America, the practice of dropping pamphlets behind enemy lines, or characters such as the infamous Lord Haw-Haw of World War II.

As online communication became increasingly common, multiple groups realized they could take advantage of this new battlefield, where likes, retweets, down- and up-votes stood in for bullets, missiles, and bombs. When done correctly, modern information warfare doesn't feel like war; the targets feel they have organically generated their own conclusions, even as they share talking points, memes, and statements created abroad, specifically to capture their interest. The goal is to create a state of information control, manipulating the knowledge a given opponent can access.

China's infamous 50 Cent Party and Internet Water Armies were two of the first recognized "government trolls," and they're still around today.[14] These operations, which exist in numerous countries, have evolved at a staggering pace. There's no real need to rely on shouting propaganda out into the larger ecosphere of a Twitter or a Facebook—currently state-sponsored online propaganda can target an audience and a cause with astonishing precision, and, when successful, they can also control the flow of conversation, redirecting from one issue to focus on another. In China in particular, these enterprises were also tasked with operating on the domestic front, helping to shore up the image of the government, decrease dissent, and monitor conversations counter to the aims of the Party. While some tactics of online information wars may seem abstract, just a bunch of ones and zeros dashing around in the digital cloud, they can and do have proven, real-world consequences.

The prevalence of this type of information warfare came to widespread attention after the 2016 US election, during which the Russian government spread false information via social media in an attempt to sow chaos and possibly sway the election toward Donald Trump. (An attempt that was, arguably, successful.) US investigators traced this information warfare to a Saint Petersburg–based group called the Internet Research Agency (IRA), which used false identities and targeted misinformation campaigns to

---

[14] These two terms describe a broad number of operations, with the first evidence of them believed to have emerged in 2004.

131

foment domestic dissent and instability in the United States, then boosted their signal through paid promotions.

While intelligence agencies would eventually conclude that Russian forces did not actually alter votes that were cast during the election, they did find evidence that Russia targeted voter registration systems and state websites in at least twenty-one states leading up to Election Day. In some cases, they fully compromised the states' systems, stealing the personal information of hundreds of thousands of voters. In 2018, the US took legal action, indicting thirteen Russian nationals for several crimes including fraud and "impairing the lawful functions" of the Federal Election Commission, the Department of Justice, and the Department of State.[15] The Senate Intelligence Committee issued a report largely supporting these allegations, stating that Russian forces engaged in cyberespionage, distributing thousands of messages across all popular Western social media platforms, targeting minorities as well as right-wing conservatives. Sometimes these "sock-puppet" accounts purported to be everyday US residents; other times they were fake groups with names like "Woke Blacks" on Instagram or "South United" on Facebook.

The IRA also wasn't content to restrict its work to the digital sphere. Reports confirm it remained active after the 2016 election, stirring unrest in one case by fomenting two conflicting demonstrations in New York City— one in support of the newly elected President Trump and one against. In the process, they are believed to have gathered the names of more than one hundred real Americans who they reached out to for help organizing these demonstrations.

According to court documents, the IRA was eventually so successful that some US businesses began paying Russian accounts to run promo campaigns for them—anywhere from twenty-five to fifty dollars per post. It's reasonable to assume most of these businesses didn't know whom they

---

[15] This indictment was released on February 16, 2018 by the Special Counsel's Office.

were paying. As with advertising and other civilian propaganda, weaponized information quickly became an unavoidable fact of modern life online.

This, then, is a broad sketch of the history of propaganda, from ancient times to the present day. And whether you welcome these approaches or find them inherently unethical, information warfare is virtually certain to continue, evolving to increasingly unprecedented levels of sophistication.

So, what can we expect next?

THE PRESENT AND THE FUTURE

WHILE THE WORLD OF PROPAGANDA and online warfare is certainly filled to the brim with conspiracy, misinformation, and tall tales, the information age isn't all bad. The same technology that allows disinformation campaigns to run rampant also helps activists and citizen journalists report news in repressive states, countries that would, once upon a time, have been able to violently squash an unwelcome bit of news or nip dissent movements in the bud before they gained international recognition. In some cases, breaking international news has spread on Twitter before hitting the mainstream, creating a level of media democratization that simply could not have existed in previous eras.

Yet this brings its own set of unique complications. The companies running these platforms—Facebook, Twitter, Instagram, TikTok, and so on—often find themselves at the center of debates on the nature of free speech, censorship, and accountability. Per Section 230 of the US Communications Decency Act, these platforms and their owners have general immunity and are not treated as the publisher of content posted by platform users. Additionally, these companies and platforms are able to remove or moderate any third-party material they find offensive, obscene, or in violation of their own rules. However, the controversy comes when the platforms are accused of bias, of moderating their content in ways that appear to favor some ideological viewpoints over others. This accusation has become particularly popular from right-wing US politicians, who often argue Big Tech firms are unfairly discriminating against political content with which they disagree.

This alleged discrimination occurs in any number of ways, from Twitter suspensions (which Twitter maintains only occur when a user is in violation of the company's terms of service) to content being "buried" in a company's sorting algorithm. But criticism has come from the left as well, with platforms accused of bolstering far-right viewpoints, tolerating hate speech, and more. The heart of the issue hinges on the tech companies' responsibility—or lack thereof—for the statements made on their platforms, by their users. This is a big deal, without much of an easy fix. Moderating speech on platforms with millions—even billions—of users would be extremely laborious and expensive for the companies that run them, and it would be impossible to guarantee that every dangerous or offensive post could be caught. If these platforms can be sued for defamation based on whatever their users post, they'll run a high risk of going bankrupt when powerful interests decide to engage them in expensive court cases. On the other hand, social media has increasingly become the new Main Street, meaning that more and more people are getting their news from these sites, rather than older media like newspapers, radio, or television. Does this mean posts on social media should be protected under the First Amendment? Or should private companies be the ultimate arbiters of what information is published on their platforms?

The debate rages on, and will only become more charged in the future. Amid all this controversy, many have lost sight of the genuine conspiracy at work with the big tech companies. The social media giants of the world gather up a vast amount of personal information, on a scale far beyond what the average user may have initially supposed. And that data can be used in any number of ways. Perhaps the most famous example of this is the Facebook–Cambridge Analytica scandal of the 2010s. In 2018,

Christopher Wylie, a former employee of Cambridge Analytica, a political consulting company based in the UK, revealed how the two companies had collaborated to gather the data of millions of Facebook users without their knowledge, much less their consent.[16] After scraping the data, Cambridge Analytica used it to assist the 2016 campaigns of both Senator Ted Cruz and Donald Trump.

The initial step did include informed consent: several hundred thousand Facebook users signed up to complete a survey that was for "academic use." These respondents were paid to participate, but Facebook allowed the app they used—This Is Your Digital Life—to collect information not just from the consenting users but from every one of their Facebook friends. This information allowed Cambridge Analytica to construct what are known as psychographic profiles, compiling information from users' public pages, the pages they like, their birthdays, locations, and so on. Some users also gave the app permission to access their timelines and messages. Armed with this knowledge, Cambridge set about its mission, leveraging data to further its clients' aims. In the case of the 2016 election, it focused on swing voters, identifying individuals who might be either persuaded to vote for Mr.

Social media has increasingly become the new Main Street, meaning that more and more people are getting their news from these sites.

Trump or discouraged from voting for an opponent. This and similar cases show a new age in the world of propaganda—precise, insightful targeting of those most open (i.e., vulnerable) to a given message. Facebook ultimately paid some fines for its participation in the scandal, but it appears this sort of leveraging and targeting, like the online activities of troll armies, will only continue and evolve into increasingly sophisticated, increasingly subtle operations. And, eventually, you may not need humans at the helm.

---

[16] This story was first reported by the *Guardian* in 2014.

MACHINE CONSCIOUSNESS

THE FUTURE OF PROPAGANDA, taken to its logical extreme, is a future of increased, largely automated surveillance, data collection, and dissemination of weaponized information. Cambridge Analytica proved that swarms of bots, questionable Facebook posts, fake news organizations, and simple A/B testing can be automated, and when these techniques are used in concert to target individuals, they can result in a significant shift in public opinion. The marriage of Big Data and computational psychology seems, in retrospect, inevitable. The landscape of tomorrow is about nudging behavior as much as it is about predicting behavior.

Cambridge paved the way with a process it calls behavioral microtargeting, building out those psychographic profiles to create an automated propaganda department that would put the crude propaganda used in World War II to shame. Instead of broadcasting a one-size-fits-all radio program, or dropping an identical printed pamphlet over a target population, today the same message can be crafted in multiple ways, each carefully designed to best manipulate the personality of the person being targeted. Say an ad sent to a swing voter attacking Hillary Clinton for the email server debacle doesn't get a click. No worries, the program goes back to that psychographic profile and serves up another ad, attempting to leverage a different personality trait, searching for another way into the individual's head, all in hope of persuading this person, one way or another, that they shouldn't vote for Hillary Clinton.

If you didn't see Facebook ads like this in your feed, that's because you weren't the target—these so-called "dark posts" are visible only to their intended subject, meaning that it also became more or less impossible for anyone outside Cambridge or the Trump campaign to track the performance of the content. As in the days of pre-internet propaganda, the truth doesn't particularly *matter*. The emphasis is and will continue to be on what seems most likely to generate a given result. In future elections, a campaign using similar techniques could launch a massive dark-post initiative targeting a relatively small group of swing voters in a key state or district—and no one would be the wiser.

We are closer than ever to a world wherein machines can generate highly targeted disinformation at a level too sophisticated for even the most diligent, critically minded person to digest. This has motivated some experts to search for an automated solution to the problem of propaganda, leading to something very much like an arms race—a battle of bots and algorithms. Scientists like Rowan Zellers are working to create the "good guy" bots, automated processes that can identify propaganda and stem the spread of online disinformation.

These scientists will have their work cut out for them. Combatting the deluge of text-based misinformation we already face will be further complicated by the rise of deepfakes, which will allow propagandists to easily create counterfeit videos that are difficult to detect. While the majority of Americans don't prefer online video just yet—at least for news—the internet has made a massive impact on video technology and filming in general. According to a 2018 survey from the Pew Research Center, 47 percent of Americans prefer watching the news rather than reading or listening to it, 34 percent prefer to read the news, and 19 percent prefer to listen to it. Pew also found that "just over four-in-ten U.S. adults (44%) prefer TV, compared with about a third (34%) who prefer the web, 14% who prefer radio and 7% who prefer print."[17] As more and more people spend their time online, they're also increasingly watching video content, rather than reading written material.

This is where a man named Ian J. Goodfellow comes in. While you may not have heard his name before, you've almost certainly encountered his ideas. He works extensively with certain areas of machine learning and co-wrote a seminal book on the concept of deep learning—a subfield of

---

[17] Pew Research Center Survey conducted from July 30th to August 12, 2018, polling 3,425 US adults.

machine learning focused on algorithms inspired by the structure and function of the brain called artificial neural networks.

In his book *Deep Learning*, Goodfellow explains it this way: "The hierarchy of concepts allows the computer to learn complicated concepts by building them out of simpler ones. If we draw a graph showing how these concepts are built on top of each other, the graph is deep, with many layers. For this reason, we call this approach to AI deep learning."

In plain English, this means we can have programs that work more and more like an old-school organic brain. Goodfellow's most well-known invention is something called the generative adversarial network, or GAN. GANs enable algorithms to move beyond *classifying* data into the realm of *generating* or *creating* images. This occurs when two GANs try to fool each other into thinking an image is "real." Using as little as one image, a seasoned GAN can create a video clip of that person. And now, without much of a hassle, almost anyone with this technology can create videos that are nearly impossible to identify as "fake."[18]

Now consider just how much extensive video footage exists of world leaders at functions, events, speeches, and so on. There's more than enough starting material for GANs to work with here. For someone interested in, say, fomenting instability or tipping an election, it seems like a no-brainer to create and disseminate videos of political leaders saying things they never actually said. The propagandists of the near future may not have to worry about carefully cutting out the context of a given piece of video to support their claims; instead, they'll be able to generate clips of anyone saying anything, and it will become increasingly difficult for the average person to differentiate between actual statements and fiction.[19]

---

[18] Examples of deepfakes range from the hilarious to the profoundly disturbing. There is, for example, a TikTok account dedicated solely to deepfakes of the actor Tom Cruise.

[19] World leaders are well aware of this threat. In the summer of 2019, the US House of Representatives' Intelligence Committee sent a letter to Twitter, Facebook, and Google asking how the social media sites planned to combat deepfakes in the 2020 election. The inquiry came in large part after President Trump tweeted out a deepfake video of House Speaker Nancy Pelosi.

DEEPFAKES

Like almost everything that began on the internet, "deepfakes" started with pornography. Back in 2017, a Reddit user posted clips of pornographic videos with the faces of the original actresses swapped out for Hollywood stars like Scarlett Johansson and Gal Gadot. Sometimes called "face swaps," these "deepfake" videos use powerful artificial intelligence algorithms and a lot of computing power to seamlessly substitute the desired face for the original face in the video by first merging them along their shared physical features, then smoothing out the transition from there. What has made these videos even more insidious: deepfakers' ability to use AI to simulate someone's voice as well. It's one thing to put a celebrity's face over the face of a porn actress, it's another to put a world leader's face over a controversial fringe figure's face, for example, and have them saying the same incendiary words but in their own voice. The potential for a video like that to find its way onto the platforms of broadly trusted news sources poses massive geopolitical problems, so one can easily understand the appeal of deepfakes to digital provocateurs and why they're not going away any time soon.

This future is just around the corner, and so far not many people seem concerned about it. A vast, interlocking network of conspiracies to control your opinion while at the same time convincing you your conclusions are your own. So why isn't there more of an outcry? It's partially because social media has replaced older methods of staying in touch. Who doesn't want to keep tabs on their loved ones? Even if your uncle went off the QAnon deep end, you still love the guy . . . if, in fact, that's actually him on the other side of the screen.

CHAPTER SIX

COUPS AND ASSASSINATIONS

IN THE US SCHOOL SYSTEM, MANY CHILDREN ARE TAUGHT A CAREFULLY CURATED HISTORY OF AMERICA, one that frames the nation as a champion of human rights and democracy, a country so committed to this ideology that it can and will take action to bring this ideology—and, officially, its benefits—to foreign shores, even when it wrestles with its own human rights issues domestically. It's often a story of heroes, and, as such, this narrative includes many of the tropes you'll find in the hero's journey. Yes, the teacher and textbooks readily admit, mistakes were made in the past, but lessons were learned and the country is the better for this experience.

While that may be broadly true, it's a story that misses a great deal of nuance, and at times purposely brushes past some of the most nefarious deeds of the United States: coups and assassinations.

Let's start with coups. You've heard of them before, both in the annals of ancient history and in the modern age. During a coup d'état (French for "blow or stroke of state"), a faction overthrows a government with the aim of installing rulers with differing priorities and policy goals. While the term entered English in the nineteenth century, the practice itself—just like propaganda—dates back to antiquity. Many countries, kingdoms, and empires have been subject to coups, or have instigated coups in other countries. Some coups may result in the downfall of an entire country, while others focus on gaining control over a strategic region.

Many citizens of the United States have found it difficult to face up to their country's long involvement in coups, labeling attempts to understand these illegal attempts to overthrown foreign governments as conspiracy theories. Because the histories documenting these coups often originate in other countries, they are too often brushed aside or dismissed by the US mainstream media. Unfortunately, the "conspiracies" are all too often real. At multiple points in history, from the 1800s to the present day, the United States has actively participated in or orchestrated coups, conspiring to overthrow multiple governments (some more than once).

In the mid-1800s, for instance, the US annexed the Republic of Texas, despite the fact that Mexico considered the region its sovereign territory. This led to the Mexican-American War of 1846 to 1848, after which the US also took the region that is now Nevada, Utah, Arizona, California, and much of New Mexico. In 1893, the US conspired with local business interests to overthrow the Kingdom of Hawaii, eventually annexing it entirely in 1898. In 1903, the US intervened in Central America, working with the Panama Canal Company to aid Panama's secession from the Republic of Colombia, one of the most prominent examples of Uncle Sam intervening in the affairs of nations in the Caribbean, Central, and South America. In some cases, US forces sought to preserve a particular regime deemed friendly to US interests. In other cases, US leaders sought to overthrow existing governments, even when democratically elected, in favor of another regime more amenable to US political and corporate interests.

As the Cold War ramped up after World War II, reviving early-twentieth century fears of communism dominating the planet, these coups were often framed as moral necessities. These nefarious activities may not have been technically legal, it was reasoned, but they were ethically sound, and crucial to further the greater good of freedom under capitalism. From the US perspective, the world was increasingly divided into three camps: communists, anticommunists, and nonaligned countries, with the assumption being those countries in the third group would inevitably either "rise" to the level of democracy or "fall" into the clutches of an international communist order. The term "First World" initially described countries aligned with the US and NATO in opposition to the Soviet Union or other communist governments. This worldview permitted the rationalization of illegal activities, up to and including preemptively overthrowing foreign governments if Western politicians believed those governments might fall under Soviet sway.

In practice, these justifications were all too often revealed to be spurious. While many members of the political and military classes doubtlessly believed in the mission of spreading democracy, big business was inextricably intertwined with many of these initiatives, and often the idea of "freeing" a given nation was little more than a euphemism for aiding corporate activities in the region. Some members of the military became disillusioned with this pattern, most famously General Smedley Butler (1881–1940), a Marine Corps veteran and author of *War Is a Racket*, in which he alleged many of the foreign conflicts he'd been involved in were in fact conspiracies—exercises in resource extraction and racketeering.[1]

---

[1] Smedley Butler, *War Is a Racket* (New York: Round Table Press, 1935).

In an interview with *Common Sense*, a socialist magazine of the day, the retired general referred to himself as a "gangster for capitalism," claiming that American interventions were ultimately meant to help the bottom line of banking houses, oil interests, fruit companies, and the like. This was a far cry from the reasons cited in the patriotic, idealistic speeches used to sell the American public on US foreign policy. As a prolific public speaker and activist, Butler garnered massive support from veterans, leading multiple protests (and making no shortage of powerful enemies along the way). In time, he found himself embroiled in one last conspiracy: the Business Plot.

THE THREE-WORLD MODEL

The idea of the geopolitical sphere split into three worlds is a now-anachronistic Western construction meant to distinguish the good guys ("First World") from the bad guys ("Second World") from everything still up for grabs ("Third World") during the Cold War.* As the world continued to shift and realign in the second half of the twentieth century, however, the split could be more accurately described as democratic-capitalist states, communist-industrial states, and weak equatorial states with massive natural resources and/or strategic sea ports.

FIRST WORLD	SECOND WORLD	THIRD WORLD
United States, Canada, United Kingdom, Ireland, Western Europe, Scandinavia, Australia, New Zealand, Japan, South Korea, Turkey, Israel, Iran, South Africa.	Soviet Union, China, Cuba, North Korea, Vietnam, Hungary, Poland, Bulgaria, the former Czechoslovakia and Yugoslavia, and related Eastern bloc nations.	Mexico, Central America, South America, nearly all of the Middle East, most of the African continent, India, and most of Southeast Asia.

* This is an approximate, cumulative list of nations and regions assigned to each sphere. With the end of the Cold War in 1991 and a decade of independence movements that followed, the Three-World Model was abandoned and geopolitical nomenclature shifted to "developed" and "developing."

In 1934, Butler stated he had been approached by agents representing a cabal of massively powerful business tycoons[2] who sought to take his expertise in coups to American shores. Furious at then-President Franklin D. Roosevelt's New Deal policies, these businessmen wanted to stage a coup of their own, overthrowing the government and installing a new fascist regime in its place. At this time, fascism was an increasingly popular ideology for the ruling class of private industry in the US. Butler alleged this group had asked him to lead a private army of a half-million men. His concerns were treated seriously, and he eventually spoke to a committee of Congress convened to explore whether the story was true. The committee was able to confirm some of Butler's claims in their final report, where they noted:

> In the last few weeks of the committee's official life it received evidence showing that certain persons had made an attempt to establish a fascist organization in this country.... There is no question that these attempts were discussed, were planned, and might have been placed in execution when and if the financial backers deemed it expedient.

Yet no further investigations followed. No one was ever prosecuted. The media of the time, itself often controlled by the same wealthy class, was quick to dismiss the story. Today, historians still go back and forth over how much of Butler's tale was true, and his warnings about what he saw as the hidden motivation for American adventurism abroad are often ignored. But, were he alive today, it would likely not surprise Smedley Butler to learn the pattern he pointed to in *War Is a Racket* continues.

---

[2] Butler was contacted by Gerald MacGuire, a member of the American Legion, who claimed to be serving the interests of the newly formed political lobbying group the American Liberty League. This organization claimed to have no connection to Gerald MacGuire and denied the allegations of a plot to overthrow the Roosevelt administration.

In *Killing Hope: US Military and CIA Interventions since World War II*,[3] author William Blum meticulously outlines and explores some fifty-five different cases of US efforts in this regard, each of which aimed to overthrow foreign governments, and most of which, he finds, were in fact democratically elected. It is tragically accurate to note that the "freedom, liberty and security" the US claimed to fight for was often little more than the freedom, liberty, and security of US-backed corporations to do as they wished once a new government was installed, reaping massive profits while avoiding the threat of nationalization.[4] These conspiracies were all genuine, and as time marched on, more and more evidence came to light to prove them so. The coup of Guatemala in 1954 is a textbook example of the process.

In 1954, the Boston-based United Fruit Company was increasingly concerned about the political leadership of Guatemala. Ten years before, the people of the country had risen up on their own to overthrow the military dictatorship of Jorge Ubico. This was, simply put, a bummer for the leaders of United Fruit, who got along famously with Ubico's government. This company thrived off the agricultural trade, particularly bananas. In 1950, just a few years before the revolution, their annual profits were twice as large as the revenue of Guatemala's entire government.[5] The company was also the largest single landowner in the country, and wielded de facto control of Guatemala's only Atlantic port, creating another hefty revenue stream from international trade. Almost no part of this profit trickled down to the common workers, who often were treated as little more than serfs.

Almost no part of United Fruit's profit trickled down to the common workers, who often were treated as little more than serfs.

---

[3] William Blum, *Killing Hope: US Military and CIA Interventions since World War II* (Monroe, ME: Common Courage Press, 1995).

[4] Nationalization is the forced takeover of a business or entire industry by a government.

[5] United Fruit Company revenues in 1950 were around $65 million. That's equivalent to almost $738 million in 2021.

Guatemala's revolutionaries were well aware of United Fruit's practices, which included discriminatory actions against impoverished native workers, interference in domestic politics, and draconian economic practices. The new ruler, President Juan José Arévalo, instituted progressive reforms—things like a minimum wage, more voting rights, and other moves that curtailed some of the common labor exploitation practices United Fruit depended on for profit. United Fruit felt it was being specifically targeted—new labor laws meant workers could strike if their demands for better treatment weren't met (United Fruit had ignored multiple strikes in the past). The next Guatemalan president, Jacobo Árbenz, took things further after his election in 1951. He instituted land reforms, which granted property to the impoverished. The Guatemalan government's Decree 900 stated that all idle, or uncultivated land, could be part of this reform. According to the government, United Fruit had cultivated only some 15 percent of the 550,000 acres it owned, meaning the other 85 percent was up for grabs. This, again, posed a threat to United Fruit's bottom line. The company was at an existential crossroads. United Fruit's once unassailable stranglehold on the economy of Guatemala was eroding. The politicians they had bought were no longer relevant, and the nation they once ruled in all but name was closer and closer to showing them the door.

They needed help, and they needed it quickly.

Luckily for United Fruit, intervention was an easy sell to Uncle Sam. The US government was also not a fan of political developments in Guatemala, and the White House was worried the empowerment of Guatemala's workers signaled a slide into socialism and communism. This fear only intensified when Árbenz officially legalized the Guatemalan Party of Labor, a communist political party. (It's important to note that Guatemalan leaders at the time saw themselves as antidictator, not necessarily communist, in ideology.)

United Fruit went into a lobbying overdrive, bending the ear of politicians and the president. US politicians berated the new Guatemalan government for failing to protect the interests of United Fruit and other Western companies. Guatemala responded that, in its opinion, those companies—and United Fruit in particular—were by far the main obstacle to progress in its nation. By the time Truman was out and Eisenhower was elected in 1952, the figurative writing was on the wall. Tensions escalated. Árbenz showed no signs of returning his country to the easily exploited state of a dictatorship. Eisenhower's staff, particularly John Foster Dulles and Allen Welsh Dulles, urged intervention.[6] While the specter of communism was a convenient cover, the consensus in Washington's back rooms was that United Fruit, and its shareholders, must be protected.

In 1953, the Guatemalan government expropriated 200,000 acres of land from United Fruit, offering the company compensation totaling more than twice what the company had originally paid. This hefty profit did not mollify United Fruit's executives. Nevertheless, Guatemala continued to reclaim more of UFC's uncultivated land. In a hilarious turn of events, it began to base its offered compensation on UFC's own previous valuations of the property. This was even more unsatisfactory for UFC, because for years the company had been screwing over the Guatemalan tax system by massively undervaluing its own land. In a way, you could say United Fruit swindled itself.

As Guatemala and UFC wrangled over land expropriation, a massive lobbying effort began with master propagandist Edward Bernays (as we learned in chapter 5, Bernays is hailed as the father of public relations, a sort of Sith Lord of information control) orchestrating a campaign to paint United Fruit as the undeserving victim of a merciless, hardline communist government. Bernays commissioned a bizarre report—a smear piece— that he circulated through Congress. The report painted a frightening picture of a new, dangerously communist regime on the rise in Guatemala. All in all, United Fruit spent about $500,000 selling America and its rulers on the coup d'état.

---

[6] The New York law firm Sullivan and Cromwell represented the United Fruit Company. John Foster Dulles, who served as US secretary of state from 1953 until 1959, was also a partner at Sullivan and Cromwell. John's brother, Allen Welsh Dulles, served as director of the Central Intelligence Agency from 1953 until 1961.

SAM THE BANANA MAN

In their capacity as arguably the largest fruit purveyors in the world, the United Fruit Company and its antecedents acted very much like a conquering force inside Central America, gobbling up and razing vast swaths of land in order to turn them into banana fields. It was an approach to economic dominance that mirrored the approach of the man who eventually become the company's president. A Russian-Jewish immigrant who emigrated to Selma, Alabama in 1891 at the age of fourteen, Samuel Zemurray, aka Sam the Banana Man, jumped into the fruit game with both feet when he bought his first load of bananas in 1895, turning a $150 investment into a six-figure net worth by the time he was 21 years old. Over the next fifty years, he would buy up thousands of acres of arable land in Honduras, Nicaragua, Guatemala, Costa Rica, Panama, and Ecuador. In 1910, he would personally finance and outfit a coup in Honduras, right under the nose of the US State Department, sailing the previously exiled Honduran president back to his country on a decommissioned naval vessel out of the Mississippi Sound. Twenty years later, in the grips of the Great Depression, he would initiate a coup of a different type—this one in the boardroom— when he took his personal ownership interests in United Fruit (which he'd acquired after UFC merged with his company Cuyamel Fruit Co) and combined it with the proxies of enough disenchanted United Fruit shareholders to seize control of the company. Control he would not effectively relinquish for the rest of his life.

It was money well spent. After a false start in 1952 with an operation called PBFortune, which failed because the CIA was caught attempting to interfere with Guatemala by other factions of the US government, the CIA and United Fruit were able to launch Operation PBSuccess just a few years later, in 1954. This was a genuine, successful conspiracy on the part of the

CIA and the United Fruit Company to overthrow the democratically elected government of Guatemala. The information war in the US evolved into military action. The US government trained insurgents, provided arms, and also received a list of people who would be murdered or exiled. In the aftermath of the coup, Guatemala went on to be ruled by a string of US-backed military dictators leading up to the Guatemalan Civil War, which ended only in 1996. The ramifications of this coup echo throughout Guatemala today. This is only one example of a successful coup on the part of the US government, though it is perhaps most notable for the amount of information available to the public about how this operation occurred.

The United Fruit Company survived. It prospered. It exists today, rebranded as Chiquita Brands International. The company still sells bananas and remains controversial due to a number of shady activities, including things like allegedly paying off foreign terrorist groups.

All in all, experts like William Blum estimate the US has attempted to overthrow various world governments at least fifty-seven times since the end of World War II. It hasn't always been successful, but its track record isn't short on big wins. Blum states there have been no fewer than thirty-five successful US-backed coup d'états, thirty-seven if you count three interventions in Laos as separate incidents. Were these victories for democracy and blows against the bogeyman of communism? Or is the ideological Overton window dressing of freedom and liberty just that, a disguise draped over the real motivation—the expansion of capitalism and the growth of corporate profits? It's a question historians continue to analyze, and while each case carries its own set of complications and intervening factors, they all share a similar theme: while the US has, for a very long time, articulated a clear aspiration for a liberal, democratic world, it has often shown little compunction about making this vision a reality. Laws can and should be respected ... so long as they don't get in the way of that greater good, however vaguely defined.

ASSASSINATIONS

IN THE EARLY DAYS OF 2020, National Public Radio found themselves at the heart of a strange controversy. When the US targeted Iranian general Qasem Soleimani in January of that year, news organizations were seriously concerned over how best to describe the US role in the general's death. In common usage, "murder" means to kill someone, but legally it means an "unlawful" killing. The US operation had all the hallmarks of an assassination, but still, some audience members objected when NPR used the phrase. It's controversial. Many people don't like to think of the "good guys" using assassins.

Assassination is a uniquely awful form of murder. It is defined by target, motivation, and tactics. The target is typically a prominent public figure, and while the assassin themselves may be in it only for the money, the people orchestrating the assassination typically have larger sociopolitical aims—regime change, for example. While a robber may murder a cashier in the course of a crime, they're not doing so with the goal of changing public discourse or a nation's government.

But someone who fatally attacks the president of the United States is an assassin. This distinction may seem like a trivial game of semantics, but it's a big deal. In some cases, it can have legal implications.

Politically motivated killings are familiar to cultures across the planet and throughout the ages. From John Wilkes Booth to Locusta the Poisoner, you don't have to look far to find historical records of assassins. *The Encyclopedia of Assassinations* by Carl Sifakis explores both attempted and successful assassinations throughout human history and across the planet.

The term "assassin" dates back to a real, ancient organization known as the Order of Assassins. A great deal of the stories about this order are either fancifully embellished or outright fabricated. Their fortress was conquered in 1256, and their records were destroyed, so no accounts from the order itself exist in the modern day. Much of the contemporaneous writing about the Assassins comes from their enemies, such as Syrian Sunni chroniclers. These accounts are biased because the Syrian Sunnis despised the Assassins (for good reason).[7]

However, we do know a few things for certain: between 1090 and 1275, a small Shia sect called the Nizari Isma'ili, located high in the mountains of Persia and Syria, went into the murder business. The sect was founded by Hassan-i Sabbah, who referred to his followers as *Asāsiyyūn*, which means "people who are faithful to the foundation [of the faith]." They were based in a fortress called Alamut Castle, about 130 miles from modern-day Tehran. The Nizari Isma'ili sought to challenge the Seljuk Turks, Sunni Muslims who were in control of Persia at the time. This is when the group first became known as the "Hashshashin." This group actively, and covertly, murdered Muslim and Christian leaders throughout the Middle East who were deemed to be enemies of the state or the order. While "Assassins" typically refers to the entire sect, only a select group of disciples known as the *fida'i* actually engaged in conflict. The Nizari did not have a standing army, so they relied on these warriors to carry out espionage and assassinations of key enemy figures. While the reputation of the Assassins was built largely on exaggerations by their enemies, the impact of this small sect and its effective tactics struck fear into mighty powers and, perhaps most importantly, has inspired imitators ever since.

So, knowing the bizarre history of the term "assassin," we have to ask: How much of their strategy informed similar activities in the modern day? Assassinations still occur. With so much new technology in play, and so much more communication between world powers, it's easy to assume that someone, at some point, must have said, "Hey, we should make assassination illegal," right?

---

[7]   For example, the connection between Assassins and marijuana use was almost certainly a smear tactic, and there's no credible link between the order and this drug.

Well, unfortunately, that doesn't seem to be entirely true. According to the political ethicist Michael L. Gross, assassination can be more or less perfectly legal. He writes:

International law does not ban assassination unequivocally, but instead prohibits "perfidy" or those acts that abuse the protections that the laws of armed conflict guarantee. Common examples of perfidy include attacking from under the protection of a white flag or harming combatants who lay down their arms. These protections are integral to modern warfare and underlie the conventions of surrender. Without them, war would end only in extermination or the proverbial fight to the death. Assassination is perfidious only insofar as it abuses these or similar protections.

So, in this sense, assassination is . . . fine, just as long as you obey certain rules.[8]

Assassination remains a viable tactic for governments for one simple, troubling fact: it *works*. Assassinations (or, if you prefer, targeted killings) have fundamentally altered the course of human history. In Russia alone, five emperors were assassinated within less than 200 years—Ivan VI, Peter III, Paul I, Alexander II, and Nicholas II (along with his wife, Alexandra; daughters, Olga, Tatiana, Maria, and Anastasia; and son, Alexei), with each murder sparking instability and chaos in the region. Another example: six of the twelve Caesars were assassinated, with

> **Assassination remains a viable tactic for governments for one simple, troubling fact: it *works*.**

---

[8] Michael L. Gross, "Assassination and Targeted Killing: Law Enforcement, Execution or Self-Defence," *Journal of Applied Philosophy* 23, no. 3 (August 2006).

each death marking a shift in the governance of the Roman empire. The most notable assassination victim in US history was President Abraham Lincoln. Three other US presidents have been killed by assassination since: James Garfield, William McKinley, and John F. Kennedy. In Europe the assassination of Archduke Franz Ferdinand by Gavrilo Princip, one of several Serb nationalist insurgents, triggered World War I.

It's tricky to say how history would have played out if these and other murders had not occurred. The stage was already set for World War I. Lincoln had already made a lasting impact on the US, and so on. But we will never know what would have happened had these and other political leaders remained alive for their natural life span.

What we do know is this: multiple countries have committed, do commit, and likely will commit assassinations in the future. The United States is no exception. Given the deeply ingrained distrust of government and love of conspiracy so common in American culture, it should come as no surprise that one of the country's most popular, prevalent, and long-lived conspiracy theories is centered around an assassination.

Who really killed President John Fitzgerald Kennedy? In the world of conspiracy lore, the idea that sinister forces assassinated President Kennedy (and, later, his brother Robert Kennedy) looms large. It's one of the most widely believed conspiracy tales in the United States, and for good reason. First, there are several strange aspects to the story—you can call them discrepancies, complications, or coincidence. Since the day of Kennedy's assassination on November 22, 1963, Gallup has tracked public opinion about the murder. Its first poll, taken immediately after the assassination, found that 52 percent of Americans believed others were involved in the incident, and only 29 percent believed Lee Harvey Oswald acted alone. Though this number has waxed and waned over the years, recent polls from Gallup and FiveThirtyEight indicate that today, nearly sixty years since the murder, well over half of the American public believes there was a conspiracy afoot.[9]

If the officials seem universally aligned on the same conclusion, why do so many people have a problem with the story? First, there are the numerous inconsistencies in the findings. During his time with the Assassination Records Review Board, Dr. T. Jeremy Gunn was surprised to learn that some of the medical evidence was dubious.[10] During a deposition with Dr. James Joseph Humes, one of three doctors who performed the autopsy on Kennedy's corpse, Dr. Gunn learned the medical team skipped some basic steps of a normal autopsy. Dr. Humes also stated he'd made a copy of the original autopsy, destroying the first document when he realized it bore bloodstains. Dr. Gunn found additional discrepancies: what he calls "serious problems" with the forensic and ballistic evidence—as well as the troubling discovery that the official photos of Kennedy's corpse stored in the National Archives do not appear to be the original photos.

These facts do not point inevitably to conspiracy. First, this murder investigation received much more scrutiny than an everyday homicide, and to a degree it's logical that it would continue to receive heightened scrutiny in the decades following. It is not uncommon for homicide investigations to have discrepancies, inaccuracies, and missing paperwork—and these problems, when discovered, don't automatically send people into the land of conspiracy. At the same time, mistrust of the government is as American as apple pie,[11] and since parts of the investigation remain classified today, that lack of transparency coupled with an ingrained lack of trust makes

---

[9] A 2019 poll from Associated Press-GfK found that 59 percent of Americans think multiple people were involved in a conspiracy to kill President Kennedy.

[10] The Assassination Records Review Board was created by the President John F. Kennedy Assassination Records Collection Act of 1992, only a year or so after filmmaker Oliver Stone debuted *JFK*, his conspiratorial take on Kennedy's murder. The board was expressly formed to reexamine assassination-related records federal agencies felt were still too sensitive to share with the public.

[11] Apples are originally from Kazakhstan.

dense, fertile soil for speculation. Belief in conspiracies surrounding the Kennedy assassination also seems to know no real political divide. In 2017, about 59 percent of Hillary Clinton's supporters believed in a conspiracy surrounding the death—and about 61 percent of Donald Trump's supporters were on the same page.

THE LONE GUNMAN THEORY

President John Fitzgerald Kennedy was assassinated while riding in a motorcade through Dallas, Texas, on November 22, 1963. After a series of intense investigations, in September 1964, the Warren Commission— named after Supreme Court Chief Justice Earl Warren who chaired the commission—released an 888-page report concluding that a US Marine veteran and former resident of the Soviet Union named Lee Harvey Oswald was solely responsible for the death of President Kennedy. Acting alone, he hit JFK with three shots from a 6.5mm Carcano rifle (M91/38), fired from the sixth-floor window of the Texas School Book Depository. Other investigative bodies agreed with these findings, and this remains the US government's official conclusion today.

The most prevalent conspiracy theories surrounding the Kennedy assassination can be grouped into a few broad categories. The Mafia killed Kennedy. Fidel Castro killed Kennedy. The CIA, or then-Vice President Lyndon Johnson, or both working in concert, killed Kennedy. On the more extreme end of the spectrum, we find people claiming shadowy cabals like the Illuminati killed Kennedy, or that the president, somehow, never actually died. It's a fascinating, deep rabbit hole of conjecture, and the theories often contradict each other on the most basic of assumptions. There is, however, one commonality: Lee Harvey Oswald, all the popular theories state, did not act alone.[12] Again, over half of the American public believes some version of these stories, and since 1963 they've never quite gone away. (And the 1968 assassination of JFK's brother, New York senator Robert Kennedy, only added more fuel to the fire of speculation.) While declassifying all outstanding information regarding the assassination would be a big step toward dispelling some of the wilder claims, it's possible that even full transparency wouldn't be enough to stem the tide of speculation. This is because, regardless of what evidence has been produced or will be produced regarding one of history's most infamous assassinations, one profoundly disturbing, inarguable fact remains. The United States *has* assassinated people. It, like other countries, likely *will* assassinate more people in the future if it deems such actions appropriate.

But the US is not infallible. Just as with the pattern of attempted coup d'états, the US assassination track record features its own collection of blunders and failures. The most famous of these was probably Uncle Sam's long-running mission to assassinate Cuban president Fidel Castro. Over the course of decades, multiple US administrations tried increasingly bizarre and outlandish methods to end Castro's life. Poison smuggled in cold cream, botulinum toxin–laced cigars, a syringe of lethal substances hidden in a pen. The CIA reached out to Mafia syndicates in the US, seeking to arrange a hit. Some of the plots focused on character assassination, essentially deciding that, if the man couldn't be killed, discrediting him was the next best thing. What if thallium salt could destroy his facial hair? Could LSD be piped into his recording studio, causing him to hallucinate on air? The last documented attempt on Castro's life occurred in 2000 while he was on a trip to Panama. His personal security guards discovered a cache of explosives hidden under a podium. This attempt also failed.

---

[12] Theorists also tend to place great weight on Oswald's own death—he was murdered on November 24, 1963, by a local nightclub owner named Jack Ruby. Ruby died while awaiting a retrial on January 3, 1967.

This list of farcical misfires points to one reason we should be skeptical of many assassination conspiracy theories. How can the same government capable of orchestrating and carrying out a convoluted plot to kill its own president—including a sweeping, multigenerational cover-up of that act—also be so incompetent that it could not kill another world leader, despite more than 600 separate attempts?[13]

Nevertheless, we are faced with the undeniable fact that members of the United States government are capable of ordering, planning, and carrying out the execution of political leaders. And this fact has led many people in the US and around the world to believe that such extraordinary actions are not as uncommon as we might think, nor restricted to foreign leaders. This brings us to another infamous, untimely death: the assassination of Dr. Martin Luther King Jr.

Born in Atlanta, Georgia, in 1929, Martin Luther King Jr. was a minister, activist, and one of the most prominent leaders of the American Civil Rights Movement. From the Montgomery bus boycott of 1955 up until his death, Dr. King fought tirelessly to further the cause of equality for all residents of America, regardless of their race, ethnicity, income, or political stance. Dr. King was assassinated in Memphis, Tennessee, on April 4, 1968. Investigations of the murder concluded King was killed by veteran and petty criminal James Earl Ray, using a Remington rifle to which he attached a scope. Riots ensued across the country.

As in the case of Kennedy's assassination, a significant portion of the public did not accept the government's conclusions, and a large percentage of the American population today considers US involvement in King's murder to be a kind of "open secret." Critics of the official narrative—including King's surviving relatives—argue that King was purposely targeted for assassination by branches of the federal government and the Mafia. In 1999, the King family brought and won a civil suit in which the jury agreed that Dr. King's death was the result of a conspiracy by a coffeeshop owner named

---

[13] Specifically 634, according to Fabián Escalante, the former chief of Cuba's counterintelligence initiatives.

Loyd Jowers, who had been hired by a Mafia-affiliated Memphis resident, Frank Liberto.[14] Jowers claimed the Memphis Police and a man known only as "Raoul" also participated. According to Jowers, Ray was framed to take the fall, and the actual shooter was Earl Clark, a Memphis police officer. The court granted the King family one hundred dollars in damages.

This ruling prompted the Department of Justice (DOJ) to reopen the case. The next year, the DOJ stated it found no evidence of a conspiracy. Furthermore, the department found there was no proof Frank Liberto was a mafioso. Jowers's own statements didn't add up, and his witnesses couldn't get their stories straight. The department also noted Jowers was being paid for media appearances related to the assassination and questioned his motives.

By the time the DOJ issued this announcement, the public had already learned about COINTELPRO. The federal government may not have killed Dr. King, but it certainly worked to ruin him.

COINTELPRO, short for Counterintelligence Program, was an FBI initiative, originally intended to discover and disrupt communist activity in the United States. The program began in 1956 and existed in secrecy until 1971. It also experienced mission creep, expanding its scope from communism to include surveillance and disruption operations against virtually any groups believed to be a threat to national security. The definition of "national security" also broadened as was convenient, coming to mean, in practice, anything the FBI perceived as a threat to the existing status quo. This included things like far-right hate groups, as well as left-wing civil rights initiatives. COINTELPRO broke laws in the service of what it saw as the greater good, and did so successfully. Ultimately, it would take an independent crime to bring these crimes to light. The American public first learned of COINTELPRO not through declassified documents or a whistleblower but from a good old-fashioned heist.

In 1971, an outfit called the Citizens Commission to Investigate the FBI broke into an FBI field office in Media, Pennsylvania, making off with over

---

[14] King family vs. Loyd Jowers and other unknown co-conspirators.

1,000 documents containing classified information, and later passed material describing COINTELPRO to reporters. Many news agencies initially refused to publish the evidence, concerned that, as it related to ongoing government activities, going public might threaten the lives of the agents and others involved in the operations. The *Washington Post* became the first to break the story, running their report on March 24, 1971. *WIN Magazine* published an exposé on the break-in in March 1972, with a piece showing the complete collection of the stolen documents. This treasure trove of information provided indisputable evidence that the FBI was conducting criminal acts, including the use of switchboard operators and postal workers to spy on nonviolent Black activist groups, Black college students, two right-wing groups, and more than 200 left-leaning groups. COINTELPRO also targeted Dr. Martin Luther King Jr. in a conspiracy to discredit his activities and, if possible, prompt him to take his own life. Perhaps most infamously, in 1964, King's wife, Coretta Scott King, received an anonymous package containing recordings of King's alleged sexual activities outside of marriage as well as a letter that King believed was attempting to persuade him to commit suicide. King believed this letter, and the recording, were the work of the FBI. In the wake of COINTELPRO's public exposure, the Church Committee[15] conducted a series of hearings and investigations, eventually uncovering evidence that seemed to confirm King's suspicions. A copy of the anonymous letter was found in the work files of deputy FBI director William C. Sullivan.

This means that, while the US denies any involvement with the assassination of Dr. Martin Luther King Jr., the government inarguably did instigate and pursue a conspiracy against him, illegally spying on his activities, conducting smear campaigns, and doing a number of—at the very least—highly unethical things to discredit his standing in the civil rights movement, and in the general public eye. With this in mind, it's no wonder

---

[15] The 1975 Senate Select Committee to Study Governmental Operations with Respect to Intelligence Activities, also known as the Church Committee, because it was chaired by Frank Forrester Church III, investigated alleged illegal activities carried out by the National Security Agency, the Central Intelligence Agency, and the Federal Bureau of Investigation.

that so many people believe Dr. King was murdered by some faction of the government, or that members of some government agencies may have had, at least, knowledge of his impending death. And with this information, it's also not particularly surprising that the jury in Memphis agreed.[16]

These assassinations are two of the most famous alleged to have been carried out by the US government, but they're far from the only examples, both in the United States and abroad. Again, consider the assassination of Iranian General Qassem Suleimani in 2020, or the numerous leaders who, like Salvador Allende in Chile, died during coups organized by the CIA. Assassination remains a viable tool for governments, criminal organizations, and terrorist groups alike. And assassinations are, by their very nature, inherently conspiratorial. Countries often don't like to be openly associated with these acts of murder, and commonly employ proxies to obfuscate their direct involvement.

The problem with many JFK and MLK theories is that theorists often interpret a lack of evidence as a form of evidence itself. If evidence doesn't exist, it's not because there is no proof of a conspiracy; it's because the proof has been destroyed or hidden by the nefarious government bureaucrats behind the assassination plot. The goalposts can continually move. And if evidence that contradicts a conspiracy theory is revealed, as in our earlier examples, there would still be people claiming this exonerating evidence was doctored or manufactured.

The latter scenario is rare in any case. The truth? It is highly unlikely the American public will ever be given full access to classified information regarding the investigations of the MLK and Kennedy assassinations. That absence of transparency, even when there are valid security reasons for secrecy, functions as high-test fuel for the engine of public conjecture. Imperfect transparency is still better than nothing, but speculation of government involvement in these assassinations will only continue to thrive in the coming decades.

---

[16] The jury, which was made up of six Black and six white jurors, reached a unanimous verdict.

CHAPTER SEVEN

SECRET SOCIETIES

"I don't care to belong to any club that will have me as a member."

—Groucho Marx, as quoted by Arthur Sheekman,
The Groucho Letters, 1967

WHO DOESN'T WANT TO BE PART OF THE IN-CROWD? HUMAN BEINGS LOVE EXCLUSIVITY. You see it in schools, where children sort themselves into cliques based on common interests, talents, or goals. You see it in the history of conflict, where countless people have died due to ideological or religious differences that can often seem obscure and irrelevant to outsiders. You see it in academia, where disputes over an arcane point of interpretation can launch a thousand ships of discourse, prompting multigenerational schools of thought in direct opposition.

F or better or worse, we all want to feel like a part of something bigger than ourselves. We like having an "in." Secret societies are the bread, butter, and adrenochrome of conspiratorial thought. That ancient impulse toward exclusivity and advantage, toward *belonging* to something, is both inherent and universal.[1] Secret societies, as a concept and practice, are real, though not always in the ways we think they are. In fact, many of the stories surrounding these groups are myths. Which, for some members of secret societies, is just fine, since some of these tall tales may well have been created by them.

The majority of conspiracy theories concerning secret societies and shadowy cabals share one common theme: exclusion. And, through that exclusion, the aggregation of power. This power can be defined any number of ways, depending on which particular story you're talking about. Some groups may, according to the lore, seek massive financial power; others, control over the rest of the world's population; still others, longevity or immortality. Since the majority of the public knows very little about the inner workings of actual secret societies, it's no surprise that tall tales often take the place of facts.

The most extreme versions of this dynamic propose that members of European and Middle Eastern aristocracy are part-extraterrestrial, part-lizard people, cartoonishly involved in any number of atrocities, and somehow super into hiding their powers from the public. Another one, popular in the United States during the 1800s, held that the Freemasons, a fraternal order originating in stonecraft guilds of the European Middle Ages,[2] controlled the country. An entire political movement rallied around this idea

---

[1] If you imagine walking into a "conspiracy-themed" restaurant, secret societies are sort of like the salsa and chips as you sit to peruse the menu. They just sort of show up, no matter what you plan to order.

[2] The history of groups considered Ancient Free and Accepted Masons is, often, self-reported and therefore a bit difficult to confirm independently. Historians trace the roots to this point.

not once but twice, calling themselves the Anti-Masonic Party both times.[3] When former Mason William Morgan disappeared under sketchy circumstances in 1826, the original Anti-Masonic Party alleged Freemasons had murdered him and used their power to cover up the truth. Freemasons, they argued, were a secret, widely connected elite, controlling all economic aspects of society. While they were pretty much on point about the Morgan Affair—he was likely murdered by individuals who were also Masons—the Anti-Masonic Party spoke about the average member of a Masonic lodge as some sort of monstrous Elder God bent on global mayhem. If you've ever known a member of the Masons, this is hilarious.

Nevertheless, conspiracy theorists can't help wondering: What if some shadowy cabal runs the world? What if the planet's most powerful institutions are only subsidiaries for a group of unelected, largely unknown aristocrats and tycoons, who are part of bloodlines dating back to antiquity? Cue the Illuminati.

Here are the facts: While no single group of people secretly runs civilization, multiple groups would very much like to give it a go. The groups capable of doing so are historically composed of the privileged—the property owners, the men, the bankers, and the priests. These groups, when effective, include a lot of people with a great deal of power, and a lot of those people are jerks. They may not mean to be. Most people don't want to ruin the world; the vast majority wish to save it, and disagree only on the details of how to do so. These groups may believe the world would be a better place with them at the helm.

So who are they? What do they want, and why are so many conspiracy theorists convinced one secret group or another runs the planet?

---

[3] As with any popular endeavor, it is best to run for or toward some position rather than solely against another. Single-issue political movements crumble once the opposition no longer exists. The Anti-Masonic Party did eventually articulate stances on other issues of the day, but their at times myopic focus led to their downfall.

To answer this, we need to start by defining what a secret society actually is. Any secret society, whether a college fraternity or guerilla insurgency, will usually be founded on three principles.

First, *secrecy*—after all, it's in the name! A secret society is a group of people who have agreed, sometimes through ritualistic oaths, to keep their activities secret. This doesn't mean these activities are necessarily evil, or even that they would be interesting to outsiders. This also doesn't mean the public isn't aware of a given group's existence. The inner workings of a society may be secret, but the existence of the society, in general, is not.

A secret society is a group of people who have agreed, sometimes through ritualistic oaths, to keep their activities secret.

Second, *exclusivity*. Not everyone can be a member. The criteria for membership may include one or more of any innumerable factors: gender, family lineage, political or spiritual ideology, and so on. If everyone becomes a member of the group, that group, by definition, is no longer secret. Additionally, membership may be based on an invitation-only approach. A prospective member may need to have one or more sponsors already active in the organization. In some cases, they may need to already possess some measure of social influence or financial success outside the group, something that brings a benefit to the existing organization. Whatever form it takes, this exclusivity creates a common cause, a strong sense of "us," the members, and "them," the outsiders.

Third, a secret society brings its members *advantages and responsibilities*. This can manifest in a number of different ways. Members of a fraternal organization like the Masons may give preferential treatment to their colleagues: leniency in legal matters, sweetheart business deals, assistance with social or personal endeavors—favors performed as both an obligation and as an act of generosity, the same way a non-Mason would seek to help out their own friends.[4] There's also the idea that access to secret knowledge may provide advantages all its own. The hidden teachings of a society may promise to bring a new understanding of the world—to "illuminate"[5] the initiated mind, revealing deeper truths inaccessible to those outside the group.

From these three common principles, we can easily see a surprising number of organizations functioning as secret societies, even if they do not recognize themselves as such. Some organized crime groups or cartels can be called secret societies. Take the Mafia: traditional membership, the highest ranks, is based on one's ancestry. In the US and Sicilian Mafia, a "made man" must be Italian, or have Italian ancestry. He must additionally be sponsored by an existing made man. He must take the oath of *omertà*, a code of conduct requiring silence about the group's activities, as well as obeisance to certain hierarchical rules. In exchange, the newly initiated made man gains rights and responsibilities unavailable to the squares.

On the other side of the law, some intelligence communities function as secret societies. Once "initiated" by being hired by the agency, an agent receives a security clearance allowing access to information restricted from the public. While there may be internal transparency, all information available to the public is carefully curated. Along with these rights and responsibilities, agents may often, in practice, have unofficial advantages due to their positions, for example, the ability to get preferential legal treatment for a friend, family member, or associate or—though this isn't often talked about—the ability to use one's knowledge for personal gain.[6]

---

[4] Think of things like: having a fellow Mason in law enforcement keep your kid from getting hauled to jail after a wild night on the town, helping a brother Mason out with a business loan, or hiring a fellow Mason's relative for a job.

[5] Hahaha—get it?

[6] Note that this is generally frowned upon, and if doing so violates the law, agents can face serious criminal charges. However, if a government employee leaves their public service job to become a private consultant, the laws get a bit murkier.

THE KNIGHTS TEMPLAR

Founded during the Crusades to protect Christian pilgrims on their journeys to sacred Holy Land sites, the Poor Fellow-Soldiers of Christ and the Temple of Solomon (aka The Knights Templar) is one of the Western world's earliest known secret societies. Created by a French knight named Hugues de Payens, the group's members took monastic-type vows concerning their personal conduct, but as an organization they would end up amassing incredible power and wealth thanks to their decision early on to start a bank allowing pilgrims to withdraw money on their pilgrimages, which they'd originally deposited back in their home countries. The Knights Templar's star would burn bright and hot, then die the same way. In a matter of decades they were lending money to monarchs. They owned the island of Cyprus and their own navy, both of which were recognized and protected by the Papacy. But in the early 1300s, they ran afoul of Phillip IV, the king of France, to whom they refused to lend money. Phillip responded by burning dozens of them at the stake in the middle of Paris, then forcing the Pope to disband and disavow the Knights Templar, officially. In the Templar's decision to focus on banking and dabble in geopolitics, one can easily see the beginnings of so many conspiracy theories that stretch across history tying various secret societies to sovereign governments and global banking.

College fraternities exhibit the traits of a secret society, as do some online communities. Political or military groups throughout history also qualify as secret societies—in many cases, these organizations resorted to secrecy out of necessity, as a matter of survival. While the Knights Templar may be one of the most famous examples, the Order of Assassins could also be called a secret society. Organizations like the Tong of the Chinese diaspora, the Crocodile and Leopard societies of West Africa, Cicada 3301, the Shindo Renmei of Brazil, the mystery religions and cults of the ancient

Mediterranean—the list goes on. Once you look around, regardless of which era of history or which civilization you dig into, you'll find evidence of something like a secret society. The world's leaders are well aware of this, and over the course of history, countries and regimes have banned specific secret societies, or banned them all entirely, due to perceived (and sometimes genuine) threats against the status quo.[7]

Establishing the existence of these organizations isn't the point. History is riddled with them, and they pursue any number of goals in the present day. Let's get to the *real* questions:

> Does any one group actually run the world? Do popular secret-society conspiracy theories hold up under scrutiny?

THE ILLUMINATI

FOR MANY CONSPIRACY THEORISTS, these questions immediately conjure the specter of the Illuminati. In the world of conspiracy folklore, the Illuminati is an ancient group of sometimes-not-quite-human movers and shakers. They are the powers behind the throne, the elite of every aspect of civilization. A casual internet search for members of the Illuminati will turn up accusations against everyone from members of the Rothschild banking dynasty to obscure members of royal families, as well as celebrities and musicians like Beyoncé and Jay-Z. At some point, these theories can seem to overshoot, leading people to ask, "Wait, are *all* influential people who associate with each other members of the Illuminati?" The answer, simultaneously comforting and a little bit depressing, is no.

---

[7] Italy, for example, constitutionally forbids the creation of secret societies, particularly any association with a military bent. This law, however, did little to prevent the rise of *Propaganda Due*, a far-right movement to control the people of Italy through terror and propaganda.

Of course not. People of similar income level, social position, and interests tend to gravitate to one another, because people like hanging out with people that remind them of themselves. You end up at the same fundraisers, the same weddings, the same vacation spots. That tendency toward enjoying shared interests is as natural as passing gas;[8] it doesn't require a vast conspiracy. But there is a grain of truth to all the legends and claims about the Illuminati.

Over the past few centuries, multiple groups have been referred to as the "real" Illuminati. Some of them are made up out of whole cloth, and others were genuine—real people working in secret to advance their goals. The most well-known real "Illuminati" was founded on May 1, 1776, by a guy named Adam Weishaupt in Bavaria (part of modern-day Germany). Weishaupt was a professor of law who searched for ways to promote what we would today call secular education. He resented superstition and the power of religion in society. In particular, he and his colleagues—who originally called themselves Perfectibilists[9]—hoped to alter the political landscape of European society, removing the pervasive hold of religion over affairs of the state.

> **Over the past few centuries, multiple groups have been referred to as the "real" Illuminati.**

Weishaupt's project shouldn't seem particularly insidious, especially to readers from the United States, where religion is, in theory at least, explicitly separated from government.

So why the focus on secularism to begin with?

---

[8] The average human being farts seventeen to twenty-three times a day.

[9] The organization's original name was *Bund der Perfektibilisten*, or Covenant of Perfectibility. Weishaupt later went back and changed the name. It appears that at some point he realized it was a mouthful. He went through a couple of different ideas for names before landing on the *Illuminatenorden*, or Order of Illuminati. (For a while, he was pretty close to calling it the "Bee Order" instead.) The guy just wasn't great at names, and he probably lifted the term "Illuminati" from preexisting Spanish ideas.

170

It turns out Weishaupt was pretty fed up at work. He was the only nonclerical professor at the University of Ingolstadt, which was heavily controlled by the Jesuit order.[10] Despite Pope Clement XIV's decision to dissolve the Jesuits in 1773,[11] they were still the reigning mean girls of the university and constantly harassed any nonclerical staff whose work rubbed them the wrong way. Weishaupt had had enough. This experience radicalized him against the clergy running the university and religious authority in general. He was, in short, super pissed when the university dictated what he could teach students. He wanted to spread the ideas of the Enlightenment, and if he couldn't do it through official channels, he would find another way.

Weishaupt and his students went underground. They agreed to use aliases when communicating with each other—Weishaupt, for example, was to be referred to as Spartacus. Their philosophical conversations wouldn't seem particularly unusual or dangerous today; their secrecy was simply an act of survival, a necessary move to give themselves the freedom to discuss things that might go against the doctrine of religious authorities.

This order—the closest thing to a documented, historical Illuminati—lasted until around 1785. Along the way, some members of the organization joined the Freemasons in order to recruit members for their own group. While it made sense for the Illuminati to expand through existing social channels, this association with Masonry later confused the hell out of folks generally unfamiliar with weird clubs. People often mistakenly conflate these two related, but distinct, secret societies in the modern day.

The requirements for Illuminati membership were pretty standard for groups of this ilk: the existing members had to approve of you. You had to be relatively well-off, have a good public reputation, and come from a decent family. As with the Freemasons, a ranking system determined your

---

[10] The Society of Jesus is a Roman Catholic order founded by a Spanish soldier named Ignatius in 1540. Members of this order are known as Jesuits. Pope Francis (Jorge Mario Bergoglio) is a member.

[11] The Society of Jesus was restored to its official position in 1814 by Pope Pius VII.

standing within the Illuminati. New members started out as novices, later advancing to the rank of *minerval*,[12] and from there, you could become an "illuminated minerval." It sounds like a lot of work, and it probably was; all for membership into what was, at this point, essentially a secret book club. Weishaupt and his followers had ideas about science and government, and generally agreed religious influence was holding humanity back. (Keep in mind Weishaupt was still infuriated, on a personal level, with those Jesuits running the university.) As the Illuminati grew, this initiation system became more complicated. Eventually, a candidate would have to progress through thirteen degrees of initiation to become a full member.

Secrecy was taken seriously. Members used pseudonyms in communication. Progression upward in the group's hierarchy hinged on secret rituals, most of which are lost to history. Seized documents from members of the group shed a bit of light on some processes, and they don't seem particularly devilish or evil. For example, one secret practice required the would-be Illuminatist to take every book they owned and summarize it. They'd also have to write a list of their self-perceived weaknesses, as well as a list of anyone they considered an enemy. Most importantly, they'd need to promise that, should push come to shove, they would put the good of the Illuminati over their personal interests.

The Bavarian Illuminati made a big splash—they targeted influential people for membership and grew to include around 600 members by 1782. Weishaupt had started with students, but as the group's size ballooned, intellectuals, lawyers, doctors, and members of royal houses also joined up. By 1784, they boasted a membership of somewhere between 2,000 to 3,000 individuals. That's a lot of pseudonyms! Yet all things, good or bad, come to an end, and this secret society was no exception. Historians generally agree the Illuminati ran into trouble in 1784, when internal disagreements and

---

12 The Illuminati's symbol was the owl of Minerva, representing knowledge. The association of an all-seeing eye, often framed in a pyramid capstone, predates the creation of the Bavarian Illuminati.

scrutiny from Karl Theodor, the Duke of Bavaria, put the organization in an unpleasant, public light. That year, Theodor banned the creation of any society, secret or not, that had not been previously legally authorized. To drive the point home, he followed up with another edict a year later explicitly banning the Illuminati.

In the wake of this official targeting of the Illuminati, suspected members were apprehended, their offices and homes searched. Authorities found documents containing controversial opinions on subjects such as suicide, atheism, and abortion. To the average person, this proved the Illuminati was evil: a threat to the religious and political status quo. Weishaupt was initially fired from his teaching position and then exiled from Bavaria entirely. He eventually passed away in 1830.

From the moment this real Illuminati began to dwindle, the conspiracy theories began. Religious authorities in France speculated that the Illuminati or its former members were responsible for the French Revolution. Early American politicians referenced the group in an unflattering light, and Thomas Jefferson was once accused of secretly being a member. Allegations that the Illuminati continues to operate in secret remain commonplace today. From what we can tell, the Illuminati was at best partially successful in their endeavors—enough to be seen as a threat at least—but they never quite reached their goal of fundamentally changing the world.

Authors such as Chris Hodapp, coauthor of *Conspiracy Theories and Secret Societies for Dummies*, conclude the historical Illuminati is a thing of the past. While other groups may lay claim to the name in their own self-generated mythologies, they're embellishing the tale, and sometimes just going for a good old-fashioned grift to make some cash. Today, the Illuminati remains popular in modern culture. The organization is name-checked in countless works of fiction, though not generally treated as a serious threat.

Yet the stories persist, and they persist because their primary assumption describes something true about our world. There are indeed modern groups of elites, and some of these groups have been accused of circumventing the rule of law to make their various dreams reality.

173

THE ILLUMINATI ROSTER

A Google search for "celebrities accused of being Illuminati" produces a list of names worthy of its own Hollywood Walk of Fame. These are just the first thirty that pop up on the front page.

Jay-Z	Beyonce	LeBron James
Tom Hanks	Chrissy Teigen	John Legend
Jennifer Lopez	Donald Trump	Madonna
Selena Gomez	Justin Bieber	Adele
Adam Lambert	Eminem	Barack Obama
Celine Dion	Britney Spears	Will Smith
Lady Gaga	Emma Watson	Johann Goethe
Thomas Jefferson	Henry Kissinger	Queen Elizabeth
David Rockefeller	Kanye West	Jimmy Carter
George Bush	Taylor Swift	Kim Kardashian

MODERN INTERNATIONAL ELITES

NOT EVERY SECRET SOCIETY, it turns out, is bent on world domination. While the rich, powerful, and well connected may sometimes seem like they live on a different planet, they're still just people. They're often stressed. They want their friends to think they're cool. They love being able to unwind in each other's company. This is where things like San Francisco's Bohemian Club come into play.

The Bohemian Club, which was founded in 1872, is (in)famous for an annual gathering it holds in the midst of 2,700 privately held acres of wilderness in northern California known as Bohemian Grove. Every summer, the club gets notable individuals from the world of politics, business, academia, and entertainment together for what could genuinely be described as a summer camp. *Spy* magazine's Philip Weiss, who infiltrated the gathering in 1989, threw some cold water on the more conspiratorial claims about the event. Weiss was able to confirm that the attendants of the Grove were indeed powerful people—the movers and shakers of Washington, highly placed executives of corporations, and so on. He also confirmed the use of rituals, most notably a mock cremation called the Cremation of Care, where they burned an effigy in front of a forty-foot-tall statue of an owl (shout-out to Weishaupt). Weiss didn't see evidence that these men were meeting in secret to lay out policy, plan wars, or hatch giant mergers. It was more like a laid-back, oddball networking event. People drank (and urinated) freely, caught up with old friends, told stories, sang songs, acted in plays. While it is officially meant as an escape from the grind of day-to-day life, Weiss heard members feeling each other out for future opportunities to collaborate—things they'd possibly follow up on in the future. To call the Bohemian Club a secret society may not be entirely correct, as so many of its historical attendees have been well known, and these days many of the Grove's goings-on are public knowledge. If you're looking for some wild, at times funny accounts of the rich and powerful a few drinks in, you'll find those stories in Bohemian Grove. But if you're looking for proof of vast conspiracies to institute a New World Order, overthrow governments and so on, you're probably at the wrong party.

This doesn't mean such gatherings don't exist. Over the decades countless international groups have been accused of using their influence to circumvent the rule of law, pushing for legislation and policies that advance any number of agendas, from stricter environmental regulations to a full-fledged one-world government. The names are familiar to any conspiracy theorist: outfits such as the Bilderberg Group, the Council on Foreign

175

Relations, the Trilateral Commission, the World Economic Forum in Davos, Switzerland, and so on. These groups could be described as, at best, quasi-secret societies. They're certainly exclusive, and membership bestows a measure of prestige. Security is tight, and while the groups do publish reports, most of the inner discussions remain hidden from the public.

The goals of these groups are admittedly ambitious. In the case of the Bilderberg Group, one highly placed member, British Labour MP Denis Healey, went on record with journalist Jon Ronson (author of *Them*) stating:

> To say we were striving for a one-world government is exaggerated, but not wholly unfair. Those of us in Bilderberg felt we couldn't go on forever fighting one another for nothing and killing people and rendering millions homeless. So we felt that a single community throughout the world would be a good thing.

This doesn't seem like a cabal of supervillains. From Healey's statement—and he should know, as he served on the Bilderberg steering committee for decades—it sounds as if this group of the international set is trying to foster global cooperation to tackle problems simply too big for any one government to handle alone. This type of collaboration occurs, on a smaller level, throughout the world of diplomacy and at international summits. After the bombastic public speeches are done, it's not uncommon for representatives of nation-states to speak with one another privately, with a more solicitous attitude, to touch base behind the scenes and say, "OK, our people have had our differences, but let's you and me find a way to work this out."

The group does include prominent people from the world of finance, and there's no denying that the matters discussed in these secret gatherings can and do affect larger public policy.

It is hardly surprising that these government representatives sound each other out over questions about how best to steer the global economy and how best to implement large-scale changes and massage public opinion into supporting those changes. Clearly something important gets discussed at these meetings, as some of the world's most powerful individuals regularly go out of their way to clear their schedules and attend.

Critics of this secretive approach have some valid concerns. Speculation thrives in secrecy, and the people who may be affected by proposals in these groups don't get to make their own voices heard. Only a handful of human beings get a chance to sit at these tables, and few among the rest have the opportunity to speak directly with these world leaders. Yet there's a valid, implicit argument in favor of the supporters and attendees: they may feel more at ease, able to be more honest, when speaking about shared concerns with their peers. And given the massive amount of power held by the people at these meetings, they are more likely to be effective in addressing global problems than a normal person.

Conspiracy theories attribute to these organizations an enormous amount of power and competence, often arguing that they all work in concert, like fingers on a hand. If that's the case, the hand in question must be cartoonishly clumsy: the Bilderbergs, the Davos attendees, the CFR members, and the like haven't stopped climate change. They haven't decided who gets to be in charge of every one of the 190-plus UN-recognized countries. They haven't silenced the public dissent from their critics, nor have they won over the support of most people. While it's highly likely that members of these organizations have participated in endeavors we would perceive as unethical, or even illegal, they don't think of themselves as the "bad guys," and they don't sit around secretly eating children or high-fiving each other over acts of genocide. From their perspective, they're trying to make the world a better place—more prosperous, more predictable, and more stable.

But what makes the world a better place? Defining some greater good depends on the perspective of the person contemplating it, and the members of these groups are immensely privileged. They will tend to have an extraordinarily different life experience and worldview when compared to the everyday populations they claim to represent: the ordinary voters, the employees, the poor. What can seem like a great idea in a speech made to the privileged few can end up, with absolutely no ill intention, feeling a lot like an evil scheme to the folks affected by it down the road. Take vaccinations, for example, or controversial economic and monetary policies like austerity or budget cuts to social programs.

SECRET SOCIETIES ON CAMPUS

WE'VE MENTIONED THE IDEA OF FRATERNITIES as secret societies several times, and they deserve a little more scrutiny. The halls of academia are familiar stomping grounds for secretive groups, though they vary widely in their levels of secrecy. As with any other in-group, these associations have their own requirements for membership, their own rituals of initiation, their own advantages and responsibilities bestowed upon members. You'll often hear a few of these organizations are too powerful. Their influence extends well beyond the bounds of campus, well past the frenetic, hurried days of college. One of the most famous examples of such a secret club can be found at Yale University, the home of Skull and Bones.

Skull and Bones, also known as Order 322, the Order, or, intriguingly, the Brotherhood of Death, is perfect conspiracy fodder. The nickname for their headquarters is the "Tomb," a windowless building with a landing pad for helicopters. Members, referred to as "Bonesmen," often go on to attain levels of worldly success undreamed of by others, even their fellow undergrads. The list of Bonesmen includes prominent business leaders, media magnates, senators, Supreme Court justices, and multiple US presidents—not too long ago the American public found itself in a surreal situation when it was revealed that both George W. Bush and John Kerry, who were running for president as the Republican and Democratic nominees, were Bonesmen. Again, fingers on a hand. In the 2004 presidential campaign, journalist Tim Russert brought up the issue directly, asking both then-President Bush and Senator Kerry about their time in Skull and Bones. The president famously remarked, "It's so secret we can't talk about it," and Kerry, despite being Bush's political opponent, appeared to have his back when he said, "You trying to get rid of me here?"

Conspiracy theories about this group tend to emphasize the possibility for backroom political or corporate collusion on the part of the Bonesmen—essentially, nepotism on steroids. This is not an unfair accusation. Fraternities commonly require their members to issue a pledge of support for their colleagues, and for many people these relationships often lead to lifelong friendships. It's not uncommon—in fact, it's expected—that members of fraternities will reach out to others if they need a hand with a specific issue, such as finding a job, getting a loan, or obtaining an invitation to an exclusive soiree. And, again, none of that is inherently illegal.

The problem: this nepotism can be distorted when the people involved also have access to massive financial wealth, when they sit at the seats of power. It's not uncommon to, say, help a friend or family member land an interview for a job. But most of us don't live in a world where our friends can appoint us to the board of a world-class nonprofit, or provide us access to a politician, or make us an executive at an international corporation. That level of influence and access simply isn't within the reach of anyone but a privileged few. While being a member of a prestigious, privileged fraternity doesn't automatically mean a person is engaging in conspiracy, corruption, or crime, it would be ridiculous to pretend the *opportunity* to do so, and the *likelihood* of getting away with it, somehow does not exist. Of course, as any member of a fraternity or sorority can assure you, these groups aren't some sort of hidden army waiting to overthrow the government, force people into slavery, or take over the planet. They're groups of, in theory, friends who want to help each other live better lives, attain success, and carry on their traditions.

Yet the more powerful a given fraternity is, the deeper its network extends, the more plausible those opportunities for corruption become.

That's the next piece of the puzzle. Exclusivity, and through exclusivity, power. When secret societies go bad, that power can lead to a world in which the laws of the land aren't applied equally. Power becomes a kind of qualified immunity.

The power of these unofficial networks can lead one to wonder: *Why should people I didn't elect, appoint, or approve of get to make decisions that personally affect me?* It's a crucial question, one human societies have grappled with, unsuccessfully, for thousands of years. The problem is inherent in all types of political organizations. It's common in monarchies and dictatorships, of course, but as we have seen, it is also prevalent in different types of elected representative governments, from the ancient past to the modern day. In the twenty-first century US, one of the newest iterations of this pattern and all the concerns it invokes is called the "Deep State."

THE DEEP STATE RABBIT HOLE

IN CONSPIRACY THEORIES about the Deep State, elected officials are often thought of more as paid actors than working politicians. In this view, politicians use most of their time to get the agenda of their powerful patrons passed, going on TV to make speeches about whatever they're told to say that week or doing backroom deals with other bought-off pols. If their puppet masters don't have anything pressing at the time, the politicians might focus on whatever the latest polls show them will best increase their chances of getting reelected when it's time for the campaign circus to start again.

But who are these mysterious masters? According to some conspiracy theorists, an insidious cabal exists behind the curtain. It's a group separate from the well-heeled kingmakers of campaign donations. The members of this group may be somewhat familiar to the public, but most of them don't hold the kind of positions garnering media spotlights. They're hired or appointed, rather than elected, and their careers continue from one administration to the next. A Republican president might lose their reelection bid, and a Democratic administration might take the public reins, but old John Q. Shadow (or whomever) down there in the bowels of the CIA or the NSA doesn't take much notice. He doesn't need to. He's been quietly working in both the private and public spheres for decades. He has, by virtue of his experience and position, access to information beyond that of the latest senators or president—the kind of stuff considered "need to know only." He and his colleagues in the Deep State have confidential agendas and long-term plans that will proceed, largely undisturbed, no matter who is in Congress or the White House. And these plans will carry on unabated after this new administration leaves office. This cabal, through any number of proxies and front organizations, has already decided who will helm that next administration. Its number one priority in selecting this next president is making sure that, by hook or by crook, the guy up next will play ball and, in general, stay out of the way.

Anyone with a passing knowledge of QAnon theories is doubtlessly familiar with the concept of a Deep State—the belief that true governmental power does not lie with elected officials but rather with unelected members of the corporate and political class. These individuals, according to the theory, tend to stay in power regardless of administration or political party. And their influence, not that of Congress or the executive branch, determines the actions of the United States.

Anyone with a passing knowledge of QAnon theories is doubtlessly familiar with the concept of a Deep State.

Good news: the influence of these individuals is greatly exaggerated. Yes, there are "lifers" in the ranks of government operating outside the partisan political churn. After all, it would be chaos if government institutions were staffed with political zealots who got hired or fired each time a new administration takes over. Over 20 million Americans work in the public sector, the vast majority of whom are unelected. No one's holding a town hall to figure out who gets to be the newest employee at the post office; there's no televised debate between middle management over at the IRS.[13] Your neighborhood librarian or streetsweeper might get paid via public funds, but that doesn't mean they and 20 million other people meet up to make decisions in secret.

The bad news is that something like a Deep State absolutely has existed at various points in history. Factions of the US government have (and probably, in the future, will) purposely hide programs from other factions. The CIA *has* functioned without meaningful oversight in the past, leading to grossly inappropriate conduct. Cabinet members and behind-the-scenes staffers *have* wielded enormous amounts of unofficial power. Various factions of the US government *have* committed crimes with little to no lasting consequence for the perpetrators. In most cases, the government employees involved aren't perfidious ringleaders of a grand conspiracy—they're just people with jobs. Sometimes their job descriptions might sound important, and sometimes they might sound insignificant, but their actual work, titles aside, is invaluable to the continuation of day-to-day life. Many civilians and members of the military spend decades at their respective careers, doing all the work that doesn't make it into the press. While the affairs of the US are ultimately based on the decisions of elected officials, the implementation and maintenance of those affairs fall on the shoulders of a largely invisible population—a nation's worth of folks dedicated to the nuts and bolts of governance.

These people aren't monsters; they're often underpaid, overworked, and looking forward to retirement. They don't get to decide the next president in some secret meeting, and they don't get invited to Davos. They're

---

[13] Even on C-SPAN.

allowed to vote, and none of their bosses tell them who to vote for. They may be more familiar with certain aspects of governance, and they keep their jobs from one administration to the next, but no one from DC is flying those 20 million people to the capital to make policy decisions.

Believers in the Deep State argue that a tiny part of this population—our John Q. Shadow and company—dictates on-the-ground policy independent of public opinion, presidential decree, court rulings, and legislation. Most conspiracy theories that mention a Deep State also connect the alleged conspirators to other organizations, implying the existence of a larger, more mysterious secret society. As of the present day there is no evidence that any such society—a single group, controlling the world across generations—exists, but the belief remains popular.

Even if you're not part of the in-crowd, there's something comfortable about the idea of an exclusive, specialized group running the world. The only alternative, which is unfortunately true, is this: there's no one at the helm. There is no group, no authority, no collective, and certainly no individual "in charge" of the world—just a lot of people who think they should be.

CHAPTER EIGHT
POLITICAL CORRUPTION

DO YOU VOTE? IF YOU LIVE IN THE UNITED STATES, THERE'S ABOUT A 40% CHANCE THE ANSWER IS NO. There are many reasons political participation in the United States is so low, including the fact that, compared to countries with much higher rates of participation, voting is often made hard to do. (Research does indicate a fairly clear set of possible solutions here: making a national voting holiday, allowing people to vote by mail, or as in the case of Australia, fining people for *not* voting.) But there is also certainly a widespread cynicism about the value of voting in the United States. Many are convinced voting doesn't particularly matter in the grand scheme of government. Virtually everyone in the US has encountered this line of thought at some point or another. The general argument goes something like, "The system is corrupt. I can vote all I want, but ultimately corporations and the wealthy will have their way."

This common belief is unfortunately rooted in reality. This isn't to say voting doesn't matter—quite the opposite. Voting *does* matter; it's just that voting once every four years isn't enough. And while the public has a well-established voting system, another form of voting exists. It isn't limited to every two or four years. It doesn't hinge on public debates, viral news headlines, or nifty slogans. It's perfectly legal, it's taking place today in state capitols across the country, and odds are you have no say in it. This shadow system of influencing government policy—up to and including writing actual laws—is known as *lobbying*.

How did we get here, and what place does lobbying have in a book about government conspiracies?

In the US, citizens do not directly write laws. This arrangement isn't the result of a conspiracy per se; more a result of the massive logistical burden of asking a larger group of people to agree on anything, much less nuanced policy. Instead, citizens elect representatives that, in theory, will advocate for them at the state and federal level. These representatives are elected to represent geographical areas—a district of a state elects a representative, with the total number of state representatives based on that state's population. Each state additionally elects two senators, regardless of the state's population. This is why, in 2021, California—a state with nearly 39.6 million inhabitants—had fifty-three representatives, and Wyoming—with a population of 590,000 people—had only one, while both states still have two senators. While it's an admittedly imperfect system, and confusing to outsiders (as well as many citizens), it theoretically aims for a balanced democracy, one achieving a Goldilocks zone of representation, one that avoids the injustice of oligarchy as well as the terror of mob rule. And as many Americans will be quick to point out, that theoretical aspiration often doesn't work out as planned. Divisiveness, acrimony, and tribalism all too often win the day, with any concession from one party to another being seen as a shameful act of capitulation, rather than an act of cooperation.

There are two crucial caveats to this process. First, citizens are not *required* to vote. Second, the act of voting does not *guarantee* an individual's stance on a certain policy or law will be meaningfully represented at a federal level. You can theoretically vote in every single possible election, only to see your chosen candidate—and policies—lose, time and time again. When the process works, it means the majority of voters simply do not agree with your candidate or stance.

It's not hard to see some of the flaws in this system. Let's say you, like many other people, vote only during the presidential election every four years. Further, let's say your vote is primarily based on a single issue—you don't have a strong opinion on, for example, a capital gains tax, but you are extremely well informed about the ins and outs of firearm ownership. As the country nears election time, you're inundated with campaign ads, emails, texts, and more. Each time you read about a given politician, you're looking specifically for their stance on the Second Amendment. And you're overwhelmingly likely to vote for the candidate that seems most closely aligned with your own beliefs on this topic—even if you don't agree with, or fully understand, their stance on any number of unrelated issues, such as school funding, trade deficits, or foreign policy. For this reason, many individuals and communities in the US do not feel fully represented by the politicians elected to serve them. It's not uncommon to find people from all walks of life stating, every election, that voting doesn't really matter. While you don't have to agree with that level of cynicism, it's easy to see where it comes from.

US voting rates are often laughably low, and it's exceedingly rare for a state or district to unanimously agree with the votes of their elected representatives. Instead, due to various bugs—or, cynically speaking, features—of the voting system, many US residents find the political process is important, yet often distant in terms of genuine effect.

The creators of the nascent US government predicted this possible feeling of voicelessness in the early days of the country, enshrining into law several powerful rights through the First Amendment. These include the right of peaceable assembly, as well as the right to petition the government for "redress of grievances" without punishment for doing so. This was a somewhat radical notion at the time, and in many countries remains so today. It guarantees the ability to complain to the government, to ask it for help, or to demand it do something without fear of reprisal. No fines or abduction; no prison time, torture, or execution. If you are a US citizen, you can contact the government through any number of avenues and literally just . . . complain about whatever's on your mind. So long as you're not threatening anyone, you're good to go.

This ability doesn't mean any member of the US government has to listen to you. But it does mean they cannot legally punish you for making your opinions, fears, or desires known. And in the modern day, this ability to seek redress functions as a kind of voting all its own. A single person may write a letter begging for a better hospital in their community. A nonprofit group may call for improvements in health care. This also means a corporation may send a group of high-paid lawyers to Capitol Hill, armed with hundreds of thousands (or millions) of dollars, to sway a congressional vote. All three of these scenarios are examples of the practice known as lobbying, in which an individual or group can use their First Amendment right to push for specific policy changes. This fundamental piece of US governance differentiates it from countless other political systems like theocracies, monarchies, or dictatorships. At the same time, it presents enormous opportunities for corruption, conspiracy, and crime. It is not unreasonable, nor alarmist, to say one of the most powerful tools for American democracy also presents an *existential threat* to that same system.

Whether you're a conscientious individual, a special interest group, or a corporation, there are ways to improve your ability to "redress" a cause. Access is key. There are only 535 members of Congress, and they are usually surrounded by handlers and busy with fundraisers, campaigns, meetings, and the round-the-clock horse-trading of government. Each and every day, more than 12,000 registered lobbyists wake up to hunt down these politicians. Whether in an office, on a golf course, at a restaurant . . . or as legend has it, in the lobby of a hotel.

THE ORIGIN OF "LOBBYING"

In perhaps the most popular version of its creation myth, "lobbying" became shorthand for the off-the-books conversations held at the Willard Hotel in Washington, DC, during the Grant administration. Located half a block from the White House, just across what is today Fifteenth Street NW, President Ulysses S. Grant was known to visit the hotel and kick back in the lobby with brandy and cigars. Once people got word that this was one of the president's favorite hangs, power brokers started "happening" by and would take the opportunity to bend his ear about policy matters. Soon other members of the government began hanging out there too—and they also began receiving pitches from people who, for one reason or another, wanted to circumvent official communication channels. Eventually, the story goes, Grant started calling these people "lobbyists."

President Grant achieved many things in his life, both glorious and ignominious, but this was not one of them. This phrase most likely dates to the eighteenth century London theater scene, where a certain set of ambitious people called "box lobby loungers" would show up to the theater not for the performance but for the opportunity to commune with influential members of the city's high society before shows and during intermissions.

As you read this, numerous lobbyists are pushing elected representatives to vote for or against a given policy. And they have the means to amplify their message. To sweeten the deal they have any number of strategies, from donating to campaigns to providing trips, gifts, jobs, and other favors.

These individuals and, more importantly, the interests they represent, comprise a multibillion-dollar industry with profound influence on the laws of the United States. Corporations currently spend about $2.6 billion on reported lobbying expenditures. For comparison, that exceeds the total annual budget spent to fund the entirety of Congress. Lobbying—a largely private enterprise—is bigger than the part of government it seeks to influence. Let's go back to the example of our single-issue voter, ambivalent on most issues but strident on gun laws. This person can further amplify their views by not just voting but donating to a lobbying organization dedicated to that issue. In this case, the most well-known lobbying group would be the National Rifle Association, or NRA. The NRA has much more access to politicians than the average individual. The NRA can pool money for—and pull money from—campaigns, so much so that it in some cases it can make or break an election. The same situation occurs with issues such as taxation, environmental protections, labor, reproductive rights, foreign policy, and more. Think of any given issue, and you can be virtually certain there's a lobby focused on some aspect of it.

For the supporters of this industry, lobbying is more than a fundamental right—it's a crucial part of the legislative process. Politicians are busy people, after all, and can't be expected to know everything about a given issue. It's helpful for an expert to distill the highlights of a policy, to drill down and summarize the pros and cons, helping the politician to fully understand the matter at hand. But for critics, lobbying is little more than a euphemism for the age-old practice of bribery.

The current dominance of corporate-powered lobbying can be traced back to the 1970s, when private industry felt that slowing economic growth, the rising costs of wages, and compliance with regulation had become existential threats to their profits. Before this inflection point, lobbying was more closely associated with trade unions or public interest initiatives. When corporations entered the game, they spoke in their native tongue—money—and found a receptive audience in state capitols and Washington, DC. Public opinion matters, these business interests reasoned, but that can be nudged in any direction we choose. Voting matters, but so do campaign donations. In some cases, money holds more sway than public opinion.

Over the past fifty years, this last assumption has repeatedly proven to be, if not ethical, disturbingly correct.

REGULATIONS AND CORPORATIONS

TO UNDERSTAND how lobbying reached its present, dangerous form, we must first understand how it came into being as a reaction to policies that might have been good for the average person but bad for corporate profits.

As mentioned earlier, it all goes back to the 1970s. While the modern US resident would doubtlessly agree that transparency in government is beneficial, it's a fairly recent phenomenon. For most of the country's history, businesses spent the bulk of their political energy trying to keep government out of industry. Then the "sunshine" reforms hit. Sunshine laws are regulations mandating transparency and disclosure from governments or businesses. They make things like meetings, votes, deliberations, and other processes available for public inspection. They also require government meetings to be held with reasonable advance notices, at times and locations accessible to the public.

Like the practice of lobbying itself, these laws produced both benefits and unforeseen problems. Sunshine laws were meant to shed light on previously obtuse proceedings, allowing the public to take a closer look at what they were paying for with all those tax dollars and to discern whether their representatives were doing what they'd said they'd do on the campaign trail. This was part and parcel of a larger move. In the 1960s, just a decade earlier, a new surge of activists and public interest groups had successfully pushed Congress to pass a wave of regulatory legislation and reforms. Big business wasn't sure what to do in response. By 1972, CEOs of powerful corporations were prepared to take a financial plunge. A group of executives formed an organization called the Business Roundtable, devoted to increasing corporate influence on the world of politics. Around this time, many companies began to steeply increase their spending on lobbyists. These investments paid out, rolling back environmental regulations, lowering corporate tax rates, and obliterating proposed reforms to labor laws. The lobbyists they hired also succeeded in winning the hearts and minds of voters, convincing as many people as possible that government intervention was poisonous to any functioning economy.

The results were inarguable: lobbying *worked*. The industry and the people working within it gained power and prestige. A revolving door phenomenon emerged, in which public servants cozy up to private interests while in office, and then get a job with those same entities once they leave public office, creating a feedback loop of influence that continues today. The corporate victories of the 1970s whetted the appetite of businesses across the country, with many deepening the scope of their work in the political sphere. Sunshine laws allowed the public into the halls of lawmakers, and what were lobbyists if not members of the public? A lobbying firm could finally treat its efforts with a quantitative, scientific eye, tracking efforts and results over time. Lobbyists also championed this new era, working assiduously to prove the importance of political engagement to their clients. This process didn't happen overnight, and many business leaders originally balked at costs like leasing an expensive office

The corporate victories of the 1970s whetted the appetite of businesses across the country, with many deepening the scope of their work in the political sphere.

in posh DC neighborhoods or springing for expensive trips, gifts, and parties. Lobbyists knew they needed to speak in terms of provable financial benefits, which meant they had to make the case that getting closer with Washington meant getting closer to profits. As the trend continued through the 1980s and 1990s, private companies became increasingly active, and increasingly adept at gaming the system. Laws that once terrified companies could be rendered much less dangerous through the insertion of small conditions, loopholes, exceptions, and caveats—things that would benefit the company, while also allowing their partner politicians to benefit from good PR. Administrations could come and go, but the titans of industry quietly soldiered on, just behind the national headlines.

As the years passed, lobbying became an increasingly powerful tool in the corporate arsenal. Companies were able to play offense against the regulators in DC. When surveyed about why their agencies needed on-the-ground offices in Washington, the number one answer was "to protect the company against changes in government policy." Lobbying had transformed into a real-time game, and lobbyists needed to be available at the drop of a hat—or in this case, a check. While it's common knowledge that money can and does move the political needle, it's startling to realize just how common and extreme this conspiracy has become.

BRIBES

OBVIOUSLY CAMPAIGN DONATIONS make a difference in political conversations. If you send a campaign $12, they'll probably take it. And if you send a campaign $12,000, they won't just cash the check; they'll start to listen to what you have to say. While lobbying—hiring professionals to grease the wheels of legislation on your behalf—is not inherently sinister, nor unethical, it does present enormous opportunities for corruption. From the US-orchestrated coup of Guatemala in 1954 to the Abramoff scandal of 2006, there's no shortage of examples highlighting the power, and danger, of lobbying.

THE ABRAMOFF SCANDAL

In the most famous photograph of the disgraced businessman and lobbyist, Jack Abramoff is captured leaving a federal court building after pleading guilty to conspiracy, mail fraud, and tax evasion, wearing a black double-breasted overcoat cinched tight and a large black fedora pulled down low on his forehead, making his eyes look small, dark, and beady. (Yes, the "black hat" of American lobbying was literally wearing a black hat!) He looked like a caricature of the shady figure in a pulp novel or a film noir detective story who you see for the first time under a streetlamp on an abandoned corner at four am.

It's a fitting image. In less than a decade, between the late 1990s and early 2000s, Abramoff and his partner Michael Scanlon defrauded numerous Native American tribes who'd paid them $85 million in fees to secure legislation that was friendly to the tribes' efforts to expand casino gaming opportunities on tribal lands. Not only had Abramoff taken the tribes' money and spent lavishly with it, but in at least one instance he was accused of double dealing—lobbying in opposition to a tribe's interests to further incentivize them to sign up with Abramoff to fight off those very same efforts. When people talk about the moral hazard involved with modern lobbying, Jack Abramoff is who they point to.

Again: lobbying works. This isn't a secret. It's well established that lobbyists can exert tremendous influence on the types of legislation passed in Washington (as well as legislation at the state level). And it's enormously difficult to catch politicians and lobbyists who step over the line. The existing regulations surrounding the industry do little to stem the tide of money flooding Congress. And the expectation of favors—financial support or future employment—is only part of the problem. What's sinister about lobbying goes much further than sliding a representative thousands in donations and the promise of a plum private-sector job in the future. In some cases, lobbying firms, not Congress, are writing the *actual* laws.

ALEC

THE AMERICAN LEGISLATIVE EXCHANGE COUNCIL, or ALEC, is technically not a lobby. It's more like a lobby on steroids. This "nonprofit" organization is composed of state legislators and representatives from the private sector, who get together to draft what they call model legislation. We're putting quotes around the concept of nonprofit because it's tremendously misleading here. Yes, the organization itself is a nonprofit—what's called a 501(c)(3)—but make no mistake: its private-sector members are making money hand over tentacle.

ALEC describes itself simply as a nonpartisan, nonprofit organization dedicated to the advancement of limited government and free-market principles through "private-public partnership." Yet critics argue it's a pay-to-play system for corporations. They write the bills, and state representatives pass them. Unless you're involved directly with the organization, you as a voter have no influence on it, even if ALEC is writing the laws for your state.

ALEC has been at this for decades. It was founded in 1973 as the Conservative Caucus of State Legislators in response to the formation of government bureaus like the Environmental Protection Agency in 1970. And it's no coincidence that ALEC was created at the same time big business cast its eye toward Washington. The heads of industry saw that there were dangerous threats on the horizon, but there were also enormous opportunities. Until recently, ALEC operated like a hidden hand in state legislation. The average voter in North Carolina, for example, wouldn't know ALEC was behind a specific law in their state, and they also wouldn't know ALEC was behind a very

> The heads of industry saw that there were dangerous threats on the horizon, but there were also enormous opportunities.

similar law—perhaps one with the exact same language and phrasing—in say, Wisconsin.[1]

In 2011, journalists and activists began publicly putting the pieces together, shedding light on the inner workings of ALEC. They discovered that more than 98 percent of its revenue comes from corporations, corporate trade groups, and foundations. Each corporate member pays an annual fee for base membership. This could be anywhere from as little as $7,000 to as much as $25,000 to get your foot in the door. However, basic access isn't the same as sitting at the table—if you're a corporation looking to participate in one of ALEC's nine task forces, the groups that craft laws for politicians to rubber-stamp, you'll need to pony up some additional fees, from $2,500 to $10,000 each year. Additionally, corporations deed grants to ALEC on a regular basis. Leaked documents show, for example, that ExxonMobil awarded ALEC $1.4 million worth of grant money from 1998 to 2009.

The politicians involved also pay to participate. Each year, the state legislators in ALEC have to pay fifty dollars in membership dues. Critics claim this low cost of membership is purposefully designed to circumvent state laws against gifts and bribes. There are around 2,000 known legislative members of ALEC and at least 300 corporate members. Many of the corporate representatives are also registered lobbyists. All members of the task forces are equal—meaning that both the politicians and the lobbyists involved vote on the model legislation.

ALEC has an interesting take on this process. It maintains that only the actual legislators have a final say on the substance of these model bills. In an earlier statement, ALEC also argued that, despite the voting system

---

[1] According to analysis by *USA Today* and *Arizona Republic*, over the course of just eight years (2010 to 2018), bills based on ALEC model legislation were introduced more than 2,000 times in all fifty states and in Congress. More than 600 of these bills would go on to become law. This legislation includes things such as limiting state control over wage laws, introducing "right to work" policies, the privatization of schools and prisons, and the notoriously controversial voter ID requirements.

used by the task forces, this arrangement somehow doesn't count as lobbying. Instead, they state that "the policies are debated and voted on by all members. Public and private members vote separately on policy. It is important to note that laws are not passed, debated or adopted during this process and therefore no lobbying takes place. That process is done at the state legislature."

Perhaps the closest comparison for this process would be a high school Model UN club, if, along with the high school students, ambassadors of various actual countries sat in on the debate, and later based their political decisions on those idle conversations.

Regardless of whether you agree with ALEC's oddball characterization of its organization, there's no denying member corporations have directly profited from the laws ALEC drafts. These are not issues that politicians will brag about in campaign ads. Tobacco firms like Altria, the owner of Philip Morris USA, scored a tax break with a cartoonishly specific 2019 bill making fruit-flavored tobacco products cheaper and more attractive to young customers. Companies like Bayer and R.J. Reynolds benefited from tort reform measures making it much more difficult for US residents to sue when injured by dangerous products. Private prison companies like Corrections Corporation of America (now known as CoreCivic) hit a windfall with anti-immigration legislation in states like Arizona, laws that mandated expanded incarceration and housing of immigrants. In all cases this legislation can be traced back not to the public but to members of ALEC, who wrote the legislation as model bills.

So, a sketchy group of business tycoons, lawyers, and politicians are meeting on a regular basis, conspiring to make bills benefiting corporations, the public be damned. Representatives of these corporations are literally handing bills to legislators, and those legislators are taking those bills back home, then working to make them laws. For most people, this sounds like a pretty solid example of lobbying. ALEC disagrees, and argues it is first and foremost an educational enterprise.

While ALEC maintains this stance, some corporate entities have distanced themselves from the organization in response to pressure from activist groups and voting blocs, as well as embarrassing stories about politicians like Florida state representative Rachel Burgin, who in 2011 submitted a bill calling for a cut in federal corporate tax rates. Unfortunately for Burgin, someone had forgotten to edit out the boilerplate language at the top of the bill, which proudly stated it was created by the American Legislative Exchange Council.

As of 2022, ALEC remains active and successful. Critics hope to combat the cabal's activities through increased transparency and online organizing. The most well-known source for information about ALEC is the staunchly anti-ALEC website run by the Center for Media and Democracy, ALEC Exposed, which has crowdsourced the world's most comprehensive public repository of the bills and laws in question, as well as the identities of the corporations and politicians involved. The majority of ALEC's opponents come from the left side of the political aisle, and the majority of the legislation it finances could be described as right-wing, or, at the very least, business first. Yet regardless of any voter's personal political beliefs, this represents a clear threat to the democratic process. It's the future of lobbying: a shadow system of influence, one in which individual corporate votes carry much more weight than the vote of a single person—and one in which the average person cannot participate.

"If this is the case," any reasonable person might ask, "then why not just reform the laws about lobbying?" It's a great question, but one with no easy answer. The factors that led to the current state of corporate lobbying are Byzantine, a tangled knot of powerful interests, each of which further empowers the other. Removing the right to seek redress of grievances would also remove the right of individuals to speak their minds. Further, lobbying regulations are written by people and organizations with a massive conflict of interest. It's not a stretch to say many politicians may feel compelled to participate in the system as a matter of professional survival. You can barnstorm against corruption all you want, but ultimately

198

campaigns aren't free—in fact, the cost of running for office has skyrocketed—so you'll have to find funding from somewhere. This leads to the idea of campaign finance reform, three words virtually guaranteed to put most audience members to sleep.

For some would-be reformers, the best way to address the issue is to combat not the corporations, but their partners in the halls of government. Why not change the way Congress members interact? Why not revise the ways in which they are paid, the avenues through which they are able to realize personal profits?

The problem here is that Congress would be the only group capable of making these sorts of changes, and it's hard to convince people to vote against what they see as their own self-interest. Perhaps the best example of this is the patently absurd problem with Congress and insider trading.

INSIDER TRADING

WHILE LOBBYING IS ONE FORM OF CORRUPTION in Congress, it isn't the only operation in town. Members of Congress, as well as lobbyists, have profited greatly from insider trading. Insider trading is the epitome of white-collar crime. It's the act of buying or selling an investment based on nonpublic, privileged information. You've heard the term before, often phrased in a nebulous way, and that's because the sheer number of loopholes and caveats surrounding the issue are themselves nebulous. At the most basic level, insider trading laws are meant to prevent something like the following scenario.

Let's say you're an established business leader at Company A, which produces, among other things, cans of iced tea. You're out at the golf course one weekend, chatting with friends. You accidentally disclose your company's quarterly earnings on the green—and the caddie overhears you. After work, they hurry home to buy up all the iced tea stock they can, knowing its value will jump once those earnings are public knowledge. For some, this is just an example of someone being a go-getter. If you knew there was a can't-miss opportunity to make a buck, why wouldn't you? But technically, this is a crime, and it has been since the Securities Exchange Act of 1934.

Unless, that is, you're a member of Congress. Up until the 2008 financial crisis, lawmakers were under few real, enforced trading restrictions. The public wasn't able to learn much about lawmakers' investments or those of closely linked family members, business associates, and so on. Until 2012, members of Congress could easily and routinely use their positions to gain privileged information about any number of market-moving issues, foreign and domestic, that could impact the performance of a given industry or specific business. For a long time this problem received very little press attention, and it's easy to see why Congress preferred it stay that way: a 2010 report from the University of California found the portfolios of US senators outperformed the general market by around 12 percent on average between 1993 and 1998. Those are the sorts of returns that would make most non-congressional investors salivate.

Up until the 2008 financial crisis, lawmakers were under few real, enforced trading restrictions.

Now imagine another conversation taking place at the same time you accidentally blab about your tea company's earnings. Senator B has just received privileged news as a member of the Senate Committee on Foreign Relations that something big is happening to China's trade policy. He has learned that your company, Company A, is going to expand into a new market with tremendous profit potential. The price of tea in China, it seems, suddenly does matter. He makes a call to his cousin and asks him to quickly, quietly buy a chunk of shares so that the purchase can't be tied to him. He even, as a favor, drops a hint about this deal to some well-placed friends who have shared similar favors in the past. This is nonpublic information, as the average would-be investor does not have access to the day-to-day events of closed-door trade talks in Beijing.

Any number of strategies or financial vehicles allow the senator to do this without drawing public ire. Being in a chipper mood, he even picks up a can of Company A's iced tea on the way home, thinking, "Ah, the taste of success," as he takes a leisurely sip while catching up on email about upcoming fundraisers and tomorrow's lunch appointments. Through all of this Senator B hasn't done anything illegal because he is not an executive at Company A. Instead, he's buying stocks just like an average citizen, even though he is one of the fifty most powerful politicians in the entirety of the United States.

The 2012 Stop Trading on Congressional Knowledge Act, known as the STOCK Act, was meant to erase this type of corruption. It came about primarily due to public pressure over reports that Congress made massive profits off the Great Recession. This act aims to prohibit members of Congress from using information they've learned at work for personal gain, the same way the Securities Exchange Act of 1934 sought to stem corruption amid the corporate class. Thanks to public outcry, it passed almost unanimously in both the House and the Senate.

Almost. Not every member of Congress was on board. Three senators voted against the measure, including Senator Richard Burr from North Carolina. Back in 2008, when the public first took wide interest in this loophole, he'd reportedly called his wife, urging her to get to an ATM and withdraw everything she could, apparently due to fears of a possible investigation or prosecution on the horizon. In 2020, eight years after the STOCK Act passed, Burr's financial activities caught the attention of the FBI and the Department of Justice. Burr, who served as the chairman of the Intelligence Committee, had sold off his personal stocks in travel companies and hotels weeks before the COVID-19 pandemic laid waste to that industry and the world at large. This sale amounted to an estimated $1.7 million worth of stock, sold through thirty-three separate transactions in the span of a single day. Less than two weeks later, the value of his stock had plummeted, losing one-third of its value. (And to be fair, the stock market overall took a hit.) Just a few days before dumping the stock, Burr cowrote an op-ed for Fox News, in which he reassured the public that the US had the coronavirus situation under control. Two weeks after selling off all that travel stock, he privately warned a group of well-to-do constituents that the virus was actually going to be a massive disaster, comparing it directly to the flu pandemic of 1918.

The Department of Justice later went on to close the case without filing charges. This might seem surprising, as his actions appear to be exactly the kind of hustle the STOCK Act is meant to prevent. For legal experts, however, there were two problems with bringing charges against Burr. First, the law is new and therefore largely untested. Second, a successful conviction would hinge on a few critical factors, each of which can be difficult to substantiate in court. Investigators would need to prove the information spurring Barr's decision was "material," meaning that if the public knew about this information it would have triggered a significant change in the price of the stocks he sold. In practical terms, this means an investigator would ideally need to find a smoking gun of information in the private briefings Burr received up until he sold stock. For Burr's part, he said he based his decision solely on public news reports, which at the very least makes it sound like he doesn't pay attention during his day job. Regardless, the burden of proof is also extraordinarily high—for a criminal prosecution, the DOJ would need to prove guilt beyond a reasonable doubt, meaning that something could smell to high heaven but not be a prosecutable offense without explicit, hard proof of wrongdoing.

Burr is far from the only example of senators profiting from the COVID-19 pandemic. As the virus raged on, multiple members of Congress made highly profitable investment decisions. In August 2021, Kentucky senator Rand Paul disclosed that his wife, Kelley Paul, purchased stock in Gilead Sciences (the company responsible for the drug remdesivir) in February 2020, on the same day the company announced it was entering late-stage studies of its treatment for COVID-19. His reporting was sixteen months after the transaction. Under the STOCK Act, lawmakers must disclose transactions within forty-five days. Senator Paul's office maintains this was done in the appropriate time frame, and that the senator noticed his annual financial disclosure form had not been transmitted—meaning, essentially, he was just running late, or had an oversight, rather than intending to break the law.

As comedian Dave Chappelle once quipped: "I'm sorry, Officer. I didn't know I couldn't do that."

Why all the hubbub about insider trading? It's a clear cheat code to financial gain, and it ties directly in with lobbying. A juicy tip and a well-timed trade can generate millions of dollars in profit. It's a genre of conspiracy less flashy than tales of UFOs or CIA-run drug rings, but it's arguably more frequent, more impactful, and ultimately more damaging to democracy.

One could even argue, though probably not in public, that the benefits of engaging with lobbyists and making bank off insider trading are well-deserved perks to an inarguably stressful career of public service. While there are moves toward legislation that would ban members of Congress from the stock market entirely, these efforts have almost no likelihood of being passed. And why would they? It would be like employees of a restaurant volunteering to stop accepting tips.

CHAPTER NINE
DRUGS

WOODERSON: Hey man, you got a joint?

MITCH KRAMER: Uhh, no, not on me, man.

WOODERSON: It'd be a lot cooler if you did.

—*Dazed and Confused*, Richard Linklater, 1993

NOT ALL DRUGS ARE CREATED EQUAL, AND SOME ARE MUCH MORE POWERFUL—or dangerous—than others. After all, "drug" is just an umbrella term describing any non-food substance that can be used to affect the physiological function of the body. Drug use is not restricted to humans, as we see plenty of other animals that appear to purposely seek out and ingest substances for recreation. Reindeer in Siberia eat fly agaric mushrooms and appear to have hallucinogenic experiences. Bees can end up getting drunk when they encounter sugar in nectar that's been fermented by natural yeasts. When vervet monkeys were taken to the Caribbean from the African continent, they discovered—and loved—taking tipples of fermented sugar cane.

t's likely drug use in human societies predates the written word. Ethnobotanists like Terence McKenna believe drugs played a fundamental role in human evolution, through concepts like the "stoned ape" hypothesis.[1] Over the millennia some drugs have risen and fallen from favor. They've played instrumental roles in some religions, inspired innumerable works of art, and have also trapped countless people in the horrors of addiction and physical dependence. In recent history, the US waged a War on Drugs. (Spoiler: it looks like drugs may have won.) For several reasons, including genuine medical benefit and the enormous potential for profit, drugs have been a long-standing, inextricable part of civilization, and that's not going to change for the foreseeable future.

Drugs, and the substances from which they are produced, play a fundamental part in the global economy, public policy, and it naturally follows, the accounts of conspiracists. Conspiracy theories about aspects of the drug world are incredibly common. You'll hear folks claim the government of a given country is in bed with crime lords, or personally profiting off the drug trade. You'll hear that some drugs are purposely pushed on parts of a given population as a means of social control, or that the trade of one drug or another is the real reason behind an international conflict. You'll hear tons of stories about Big Pharma, alleging any number of illegal, unethical activities, experiments, and swindles on the part of the world's largest legal drug makers.

And you'll hear that powerful forces will discredit and murder anyone who gets too close to the truth.

It's sadly unsurprising that many of these ideas are based on real events. Government officials across the planet have collaborated with cartels, drug lords, and other criminals. Some government officials have lined their pockets with drug money. Drugs have started major military conflicts, as with the Opium Wars of the mid-1800s, which saw Western powers attempting

---

[1] While the name is certainly catchy, it dumbs down the idea a bit. This hypothesis proposes that sustained consumption of psilocybin mushrooms led to or facilitated the emergence of human language and self-reflection, possibly as far back as 2 million years ago.

to force the addictive drug on the population of China, despite the substance being illegal in that country.[2] Fairly recently, US-based Purdue Pharma was sued into bankruptcy, legally agreeing to pay out billions of dollars due to its role in America's ongoing opioid crisis. (The Sackler family, which controlled Purdue, did not receive any criminal convictions.)

Thousands died in the Opium Wars. Thousands have died and will continue to die as the War on Drugs stretches on. And not all of these deaths come from the ranks of addicts, cartels, or militias. According to conspiracy theorists, even journalists can find themselves falling victim to the world of drugs and corruption. Let's start with the story of Gary Webb.

GARY WEBB

WHILE HIS NAME MIGHT BE UNFAMILIAR to many people today, Gary Webb garnered a great deal of public attention during his journalistic career. Before his untimely death on December 10, 2004, Webb reported extensively on allegations that the Contra rebels based in Nicaragua had played a pivotal role in the creation of the Los Angeles crack epidemic. His Dark Alliance series, published by the *San Jose Mercury News* in 1996, claimed the contras funneled the profits from this cocaine trade into their conflict with the Nicaraguan government. Reading between the lines, many readers took from Webb's story that the CIA was well aware of this trade, and at times actively protecting the operation.

Webb's story—or at least the way it was interpreted by many readers—had the hallmarks of a vast conspiracy. For one, it posited a large-scale,

---

[2] First Opium War: 1839–1842. Second Opium War: 1856–1860. While historians continue to debate just how much of a role opium played in the lead-up to these conflicts, there's no denying the opium trade was an instrumental factor.

state-level crime and cover-up. The theory was that because the US government didn't care for Nicaragua's ruling Sandinista government, it was seeking ways to protect and grow the anticommunist Contra rebels. Webb seemed to imply that individuals in the CIA and DEA granted amnesty to Contra-associated drug smugglers, knowingly helping to create a system of secret funding for the rebels. This amnesty, he concluded, also meant the CIA had actively disrupted crime-fighting efforts from other branches of law enforcement against the terrible crack cocaine epidemic in Los Angeles. The reporting focused largely on three men: Nicaraguan nationals Oscar Danilo Blandón and Norwin Meneses Cantarero, and LA drug kingpin Ricky Ross. Webb claimed these men had well-established relationships with both the Contras and the CIA, and these connections explained why the government so often seemed unable to prosecute them for their smuggling operations.

Webb later sought to tamp down the more conspiratorial theories that grew from the Dark Alliance series. He tried to correct what he saw as an erroneous misinterpretation of his article by some readers—that he had conclusively proven the CIA was targeted Black communities. In a 1997 article for the *Washington Post*, he directly disagrees, writing instead that his series "doesn't prove the CIA targeted black communities. It doesn't say this was ordered by the CIA."

Nevertheless, Webb's reporting sparked enormous controversy, leading to a series of investigations into the perceived charges. Other papers said explicitly what Webb seemed to imply, and throughout 1996 the news was awash in headlines like "CIA's War Against America" or "The U.S. Government Was the First Big Crack Pusher." [3] Eventually, the wave receded. Multiple newspapers concluded the claims were overstated and issued pieces criticizing issues with Webb's reporting. Webb's own editorial board at the *Mercury News* defended many aspects of the story but ultimately deemed it "oversimplified."

---

[3]   The two examples cited above are, in order of appearance, from the *Palm Beach Post* (September 14, 1996) and the *Boston Globe* (September 11, 1996).

Eventually, government-led investigations delved into the allegations. The DOJ released a report in 1998, concluding that claims of government collusion "contained in the original *Mercury News* articles were exaggerations of the actual facts." The CIA also weighed in, investigating itself in a two-volume report that concluded there was, so far as it could tell, no evidence for Webb's claims. In 2000, the House Intelligence Committee released its own findings on the matter. As with the CIA and the Justice Department, it found no evidence that members of the government were associated with the prominent drug dealers Webb named in his reporting.

Though multiple government agencies pushed back against Webb's reporting, it's worth noting what they didn't deny. No one challenged the idea that government agencies, or groups of individuals working for those agencies, had muddied the waters of the drug trade. US officials, in fact, had been receiving reports on Contra cocaine smuggling since 1984. Back in 1986, well before Webb's series was published, the Senate Foreign Relations Committee concluded that Contra drug links could be traced to "payments to drug traffickers by the U.S. State Department of funds authorized by the Congress for humanitarian assistance to the Contras," going on to note this occurred "in some cases after the traffickers had been indicted by federal law enforcement agencies on drug charges, in others while traffickers were under active investigation by these same agencies."

US officials, in fact, had been receiving reports on contra cocaine smuggling since 1984.

The report also concluded that "it is clear that individuals who provided support for the Contras were involved in drug trafficking, the supply network of the Contras was used by drug trafficking organizations, and elements of the Contras themselves knowingly received financial and material assistance from drug traffickers. In each case, one or another agency of the

U.S. government had information regarding the involvement either while it was occurring, or immediately thereafter." [4]

Senator John Kerry, who led the committee, would later go on to say, "Some of us in Congress at the time, in 1985, 1986, were calling for a serious investigation of the charges, and C.I.A. officials did not join in that effort.... There was a significant amount of stonewalling." He added, "I'm afraid that what I read in the report documents the degree to which there was a lack of interest in making sure the laws were being upheld." [5]

The committee found the US State Department had paid more than $806,000 to four different companies owned and operated by traffickers, ostensibly to provide "humanitarian assistance" to the Contras. The claim of CIA involvement—the implication that the government actually started the crack epidemic—was their primary point of contention. That 1998 committee report mapped the ways the Contras had transformed Central America into a transit point for Colombian-produced cocaine while being supported, at the same time, by the Reagan administration, which hoped for regime change in Nicaragua. Webb's work was more focused on figuring out what happened to the cocaine once it crossed the border into the United States.

Feeling hung out to dry, Webb resigned from his position in December 1997, taking a new job as an investigator for the California state legislature. He continued with freelance investigative reporting, and later expanded the Dark Alliance articles into a full book in 1998. Six years later, he was found dead in his home with two gunshot wounds to the head. The Sacramento County coroner's office ruled his death a suicide, but the news of multiple gunshots convinced many of his supporters that someone else was responsible for his demise. Had Gary Webb been murdered? If so, by whom? In

---

[4] From the executive summary of the 1987 report by the Senate Foreign Relations Committee's Subcommittee on Narcotics, Terrorism, and International Operations.

[5] "C.I.A. Says It Used Nicaraguan Rebels Accused of Drug Tie," *New York Times*, July 17, 1998.

September 2014, newly released CIA documents revealed the agency had been watching Webb, and the controversy he ignited, incredibly closely. There was no indication of homicide in these papers, but it's clear the agency considered this a legitimate and serious public relations crisis.

For those who believe Gary Webb was correct, the story of his decline and death is inherently a story of retribution and, later, a successful cover-up. For his critics and those skeptical of the murder allegations, Webb was driven to take his own life due to his unbalanced mental state, stalling career prospects, and mounting financial concerns. While Webb may be the most well-known case of an alleged government assassination related to the drug trade, he's far from the only person theorists believe the government has murdered.

And regardless of how people might interpret the Dark Alliance today, the CIA does indeed have a history of conspiring to smuggle drugs. Let's hop on a flight with Air America.

AIR AMERICA

ONE UNUSUAL QUIRK ABOUT SECRETIVE OPERATIONS, especially in government, is that they tend to have extraordinarily benign names. To an average person, a company named Air America would sound like any other US-based commercial airline. Yet Air America, established in 1946, was secretly owned and operated by the CIA from at least 1950 to 1976. During the Laotian Civil War of 1959 to 1975, both of the superpowers of the Cold War dove into the conflict, providing significant support to the opposing domestic forces. Today, it's often referred to as the CIA's Secret War. The CIA used the Hmong population as a proxy to fight the Pathet Lao rebels, who were themselves being used as proxies for the Soviet Union. As would later prove to be the case in Central America, illegal drugs—heroin and opium, this time—provided a quick, reliable source of funds for the war chest.

Today, historians differ on the degree to which the CIA and Air America were involved in this trade. On the far end of the conspiratorial spectrum, you'll find people claiming the CIA actively transported opium aboard its airline. On the other end of the spectrum, you'll find aviation historians like Curtis Peebles categorically denying that any Air America employee was involved in the trade. A third group of historians takes a more moderate approach, concluding that while the CIA did not actively handle drugs, it practiced a sort of studied disinterest, a purposeful ignorance to the smuggling, as Alfred W. McCoy, author of *The Politics of Heroin in Southeast Asia*, put it. A sort of "well, if we can't see it, there's no need for us to really look, right?" Instead of getting hands-on with the heroin, McCoy believes the CIA both ignored the drug trade while supplying its regional allies—some of whom were well-known drug lords—with transportation, weapons, and protection from the law.

The CIA, it should be noted, denies allegations that it was involved in drug dealing. Still, an official rebuttal from an agency with so much controversy in its past has done little to quell concerns about shadowy front companies, and a hidden, international hand profiting off the same crimes it claims to prevent. Numerous researchers and former military, civilian, and aviation officials have publicly claimed the CIA engaged in supporting the drug trade not just in Central America and Laos but in the Middle East, parts of Europe, and Afghanistan and Pakistan as well. While these allegations have never been confirmed by the CIA, the agency has issued repeated denials over the decades. To a conspiracy theorist, of course, these denials don't hold much weight. From their perspective, it's only further evidence of a cover-up. After all, if one of the world's preeminent intelligence agencies was actually, repeatedly getting caught up in the drug game, ferrying heroin, cocaine, opium, and so on at an international scale, why on Earth would they want to admit it?

After all, drugs are illegal, right?

PROHIBITION

FOR A LONG TIME drug policy in the US has remained pretty static. Recreational drugs, like nicotine or alcohol, are legal so long as users meet certain requirements—age limits, for example, in the case of tobacco and booze. Other substances, like opiates, methamphetamine, psychedelics, marijuana, cocaine, and the like were considered "hard" drugs, meaning they were illegal to possess, grow, manufacture, or distribute unless they qualified for certain legal exceptions. This classification system wasn't always in place, and its evolution is a source of constant speculation in the world of conspiracy. In fact, some of the biggest conspiracies in the world of drugs hinge on the idea that the United States may have an ulterior motive when it comes to deciding if and how people can get high.

The most consequential attempt at drug prohibition in US history was the thirteen years in the early 1900s—1920 to 1933—when alcohol was banned on a nationwide level. This law, passed as the Eighteenth Amendment to the Constitution, was ultimately unsuccessful at preventing people from getting soused. Speakeasies immediately sprang up in cities across the country. They were so ubiquitous that by the end of the twenties, New York City alone was home to an estimated 30,000 booze joints. People in rural communities, meanwhile, continued to make their own hooch out in the woods, as they had long before Uncle Sam aimed to get a nation on the wagon. Ironically, alcoholism soared rather than decreased. Street gangs, once mostly centered on petty crime, blossomed into bootlegging empires. Smuggling rings proliferated. While beer, wine and, liquor, once a normal part of American life, were now criminalized, most people were able to find alcohol if they really wanted it, or at the very least, they would know someone with a connection. People made *fortunes* off breaking the new law.

The federal government made efforts to stem the flood of outlawed booze. In at least one case, they went too far, perpetrating a conspiracy that put the lives of thousands at risk. This is the story of the Chemist's War.

Banning booze for recreational consumption was an ambitious, complicated endeavor. It wasn't just a matter of shutting down America's distilleries and breweries. Despite the power of the temperance movement, alcohol was a common, normalized part of the nation's culture. People didn't want the party to be over, and if the bars pulled a permanent version of "you don't have to go home, but you can't stay here," then Americans would apply their enterprising nature toward discovering or inventing a workaround. To paraphrase Jeff Goldblum's famous *Jurassic Park* quote: "Barflies, uh, find a way." If official channels for alcohol were no longer an option, unofficial channels would have to do.

Demand for spirits exploded. People resorted to making the alcohol they could no longer buy in bars or stores. Industrial alcohol was the obvious first option. This isn't the kind of booze you'd want in your next cocktail: it's basically grain alcohol, used in fuel, medical supplies, paints, solvents, perfumes, and cosmetics. Since 1906 the US had required industrial alcohol manufacturers to "denature" their product, mixing it with several unpleasant chemicals to make it undrinkable. This wasn't a moral move— manufacturers agreed to these requirements before Prohibition, mainly to avoid the taxes levied on drinkable spirits. Nevertheless, the US Treasury Department estimated that by the 1920s, around 60 *million* gallons of industrial alcohol were being stolen each year, with criminals employing chemists to make it drinkable. Criminal empires had more than enough cash to burn, and had no trouble finding those with the know-how to undermine Prohibition. Alcohol syndicates paid way more than the government, and they were able to partner up with some of the best and brightest chemists of the day.

So, in 1926, then-President Calvin Coolidge responded by weaponizing the government's denaturing process. Around seventy different denaturing formulas were already bouncing around, posing various degrees of danger to people who might drink them. Some additives were harmless but made the alcohol taste like crap. Others, however, like methyl alcohol, were poisonous. The criminal chemists knew these substances, and also knew how to remove them. So in 1927, Coolidge raised the stakes, allowing new denaturing formulas to include chemicals like benzene, formaldehyde, kerosene, and brucine, a substance closely related to strychnine. Additionally, manufacturers were required to increase the percentage of additives, making them almost 10 percent of the total product. This initiative was, in some ways, successful, at least in that the government did manage to effectively poison industrial alcohol before it got stolen. But, in more important ways, it was an absolute disaster. On Christmas Eve 1926, hospitals in New York were swamped as more than sixty holiday partygoers became dangerously ill from consuming toxic booze. At least eight people died that night. Over the course of the next two days, another twenty-three people would also pass away, poisoned by the government. And this was just in New York—other cities experienced similar tragedies. On New Year's Day, the casualties in the Big Apple continued to mount, as forty-one people died from poisoned alcohol at New York's Bellevue Hospital. Doctors concluded some of the deaths were from drinking wood alcohol—industrial methanol—which bootleggers couldn't separate out.

The New York City medical examiner at the time, Charles Norris, put it bluntly at a press conference shortly afterward, saying:

> The government knows it is not stopping drinking by putting poison in alcohol, yet it continues its poisoning processes, heedless of the fact that people determined to drink are daily absorbing that poison. Knowing this to be true, the United States government must be charged with the moral responsibility for the deaths that poisoned liquor causes, although it cannot be held legally responsible.

Norris set off on a one-man mission to raise awareness of what was happening. He wasn't defending wild, raging parties; he was calling the government to account for its strange, deadly conspiracy, and he made some pretty solid points. First, sure, drinking was against the law, but poisoning the liquor could effectively function as a death sentence. Four hundred people died in New York in 1926. The next year, 700 died. Thousands were getting deathly ill. A death sentence went far beyond the ordinary, legally dictated punishments for getting caught with booze.

Norris also spoke the quiet part aloud: this drug legislation was overwhelmingly targeting the poor. Well-to-do drinkers, some of them the same politicians who publicly supported Prohibition, had the connections and means to purchase the finest imported spirits. They could also pay for protection from the law. Those without these social perks resorted to more dangerous stuff. Others agreed with Norris—New Jersey senator Edward I. Edwards, quoted in the *New York Times*, went so far as to call the practice "legalized murder."

The government, initially, didn't budge. People like Assistant Secretary of the Treasury Seymour M. Lowman reasoned that if the lower classes of society were dying off from poisoned hooch, and that resulted in a sober America, it was overall a job well done. The public, however, increasingly disagreed. Today, the US government's official(ish) position on the "Chemist's War" is that the Treasury Department was seeking not to murder people but to prevent illegal drinking by adding substances that it knew couldn't be filtered out by ill-intentioned criminals.

Officially, the denaturing program ended in December 1933, when America repealed the Eighteenth Amendment and the country got back to drinking in the open. Unofficially, it just sort of . . . disappeared from the news well beforehand. It left the realm of public conversation. Author Deborah Blum estimates that, in the end, around 10,000 people may have died due to this denaturing program.

Of course, shortly after this disastrous experiment in organized crime, mass murder, and forced morality, the US would go on to ban another substance: marijuana. That prohibition continues in many states today. In many ways, prohibition of some drugs can be seen as an imperfect solution to genuine, ongoing problems. Addiction is real. Heroin, opioids, meth, cocaine—as well as legal drugs like alcohol—have all ruined people's lives and come with significant social costs. Yet the future of prohibition is not as static as it once may have appeared.

Before we get to the future, we have to clear up the conspiracies surrounding the prohibition of marijuana. This plant, and the substances it contains, was made illegal through the Marijuana Tax Act of 1937, and later the Controlled Substances Act of 1970, which classified marijuana as a Schedule I drug, lumping it in with substances like heroin and meth. The original ban came about largely due to the efforts of a virulent racist named Harry J. Anslinger, who was the head of the Federal Bureau of Narcotics. Anslinger was concerned that marijuana might topple the nation's existing social order. The marijuana plant had been a part of American life since it was brought over by European settlers. Early colonials, for example, grew agricultural hemp. But it wasn't considered a common psychoactive agent until the 1910s, when the Mexican Revolution prompted a significant number of Mexicans to move north to the United States, bringing with them the practice of unwinding with some weed. This practice became tied up with alarmist cries of the "threat" these immigrants supposedly represented. High on their own stash of xenophobia, states began to ban pot.

State-by-state prohibition wasn't enough for Anslinger. He wanted a federal ban on the substance, even though most of the scientists he spoke with agreed it wasn't dangerous. Anslinger spearheaded a national, high-profile campaign that used racism to make the case against marijuana. He claimed it was overwhelmingly a vice of minorities and caused users to go insane or become violent.[6] He warned (white) Americans that, unless serious action was taken, marijuana would lead to miscegenation and a sense of superiority among people of color—in modern terms, he was worried that smoking marijuana would lead people to believe in racial equality, a view he staunchly and publicly opposed. Anslinger's campaign against marijuana isn't technically a conspiracy, though his wild beliefs

---

[6] As anyone with firsthand experience can tell you, marijuana has almost no association with bouts of violence. It has, to be fair, led to the early demise of many, many late-night snacks.

certainly had aspects of a conspiracy theory. Despite the utter lack of any evidence to support his ideas, a significant part of the population was either gullible or prejudiced enough to pay him heed. Today, several US states have walked back marijuana legislation, decriminalizing it, legalizing it for medical purposes, or allowing it for recreational use. But marijuana's illegal status continues in many parts of the country, forming a significant part of the War on Drugs.

MEDICAL MARIJUANA IS ANCIENT HISTORY

The relaxation or abolition of drug laws related to marijuana in the twenty-first century, particularly as it relates to medical applications, felt to many in the United States like a revolution in medical care, but the reality is that marijuana has been used for its medicinal properties for 5,000 years. Ancient Egyptians used it to treat vision problems and inflammation. The Chinese considered cannabis a medicine going back to 2900 BCE and in India it was used as an anesthetic all the way back in 1000 BCE. By the time Jesus of Nazareth was born, the Chinese had found dozens of medicinal applications for the plant and the Greeks had taken to using it as well. They were followed by the Romans, Arabs, and Persians over the next thousand years.

When something as innocuous as an abundant plant species has a history of healing properties as long and continuous as human history itself, one struggles to find a logical explanation for its prohibition that doesn't involve a conspiracy of political self-interest.

THE WAR ON DRUGS

THE WAR ON DRUGS IS A PHRASE, a concept, familiar to almost every American. It first became popular after a press conference by then President Richard Nixon in 1971, where he identified drug abuse to be "public enemy number one" for American society. This war continues today, and has spawned a global initiative led by the US to root out the illegal drug trade through a variety of strategies ranging from prohibition to full-on military intervention. As of 2021, the US government had spent an estimated $1 trillion waging this war. At this point it's impossible to estimate exactly how much of that money has been wasted. The War on Drugs has been contentious since the day it was declared, and like many recent American wars, it has not gone well. As recently as 2018, a solid 75 percent of Americans polled by Rasmussen stated the US is not winning this War on Drugs.

There are a great many conspiracy theories about the "true" nature of the War on Drugs. Some allege that the war exists to allow the government increased control over these enormously profitable substances. Others accuse government agencies and their members of widespread corruption. There is no doubt that it has increased the danger to professionals working in law enforcement and the military and that its harsh penalties have overwhelmingly punished the poor and minorities, wreaking intergenerational, devastating havoc on the families of the nation's most vulnerable.

Many of the long-tail consequences resulting from the war have produced actions that, at the end of the day, can look a lot like conspiracies. Before the Watergate debacle, Nixon's presidency focused largely on crime and drugs. His administration heralded the age of mass incarceration, which continues today. The Nixon approach to drug policy quietly owes a great deal to the rantings of Anslinger—it had highly racist undertones, and through associating African American communities with drug use, the administration was able to give itself a sort of pass when it came to the extreme criminalization of disadvantaged communities and leaders. Nixon's former top advisor in the domestic realm, John Ehrlichman, said as much when he noted:

> The Nixon campaign in 1968, and the Nixon White House after that, had two enemies: the antiwar left and black people. You understand what I'm saying? We knew we couldn't make it illegal to be either against the war or black, but by getting the public to associate the hippies with marijuana and blacks with heroin, and then criminalizing both heavily, we could disrupt those communities. We could arrest their leaders, raid their homes, break up their meetings, and vilify them night after night on the evening news. Did we know we were lying about the drugs? Of course we did.[7]

And, just like Anslinger, the Nixon administration ignored studies confirming marijuana did not, in fact, pose some existential threat to society. Yet the shrill alarmism—and government bloat—continued long past Nixon. The Reagan administration recognized that assuming a "tough on crime" stance was a political goldmine, and advocated for increasingly harsh penalties that eventually evolved into the practice of mandatory minimum sentencing, which removed judicial discretion and required courts to sentence many nonviolent drug users to long prison terms. Penalties for drug offenses skyrocketed, especially with the institution of the 1986 Anti-Drug Abuse Act. The discrimination against people of color continued as well, with penalties for crack use—a

Today the US, a country with just 4.2 percent of the world's population, boasts the highest incarceration rate in the world—with around 25 percent of the world's total prison population.

---

[7] As related to Dan Baum in "Legalize It All," *Harper's*, April 2016.

more common drug in minority communities—much harsher than penalties for cocaine.

This draconian approach led to a new era in the world of mass incarceration. In 1970, the US prison population was about 200,000 people. By 1994, it had ballooned to 1.5 million. Today the US, a country with just 4.2 percent of the world's population, boasts the highest incarceration rate in the world—with around 25 percent of the world's total prison population. While this increase can be attributed to a number of factors, there's no denying that the War on Drugs directly contributed to this growth, and continues to do so today.

A FINAL WORD

ANY CONVERSATION ABOUT DRUGS, whether conspiratorial, fictional, or entirely based in fact, should end with the same message: addiction is real. And although it can feel incredibly isolating, it is profoundly important for anyone struggling with addiction to know they are not alone, and countless people and organizations are willing to help. If you or someone you care for is struggling with substance abuse, don't hesitate to reach out to organizations like the SAMHSA National Helpline at 1-800-662-HELP (1-800-662-4357). SAMHSA and other similar networks provide free round-the-clock counseling to anyone who asks.

AFTERWORD

WHEN WE FIRST BEGAN WORK ON THIS MANUSCRIPT, we weren't sure where the rabbit hole would take us. This sensation—this fluttering, tantalizing uncertainty—it's a feeling we're deeply familiar with, from our early days in the trenches of YouTube, where we asked questions that don't always make it to the mainstream. When our first audio podcast came out more than a decade ago, we were likewise uncertain: Would our choice to apply critical thinking to the world of conspiracy be worthwhile, or would it be lumped in with the noise, the continual caterwaul of breathless, unsupported claims and bad-faith performance art all too common in the discourse of the modern age?

We knew, then as now, that what we were doing had to be done. It didn't need to be done by us necessarily, but there needed to be a voice in the room of conjecture and rumor, someone capable of objectively, carefully, and fairly exploring the subjects so many people strive to avoid. The truth behind a story is often much more nuanced than it may appear; that truth can also be much uglier than the sanitized narratives we're too often taught to accept at face value. But we decided long ago to follow the truth wherever it takes us, and this book represents a new step in our strange, ongoing adventure.

While we could not predict just how mainstream the world of conspiracy would become over recent years, we always knew the danger of throwing a term like "conspiracy theory" around. And we knew there were truths hidden in some of these stories—there was, at times, an ulterior motive behind moves to dismiss a story out of hand, without bothering to learn more about it. In what is often called a "post-truth" environment, a world in which the noise of conjecture, lurid tall tales, and outright lies often shout down careful investigation of the truth, this book became more than a new, interesting project: it became an important tool, a way to further our argument that the world is both understandable and worth understanding, and that while simple, black-and-white narratives may be comforting, they can also be misleading and poisonous.

In that sense, this book is a guide. It's a response to the wide spectrum of people who would either like to avoid disturbing truths or embrace outrageous, false stories without giving those claims the scrutiny they require. This book is meant to arm you with knowledge. In that sense, this book is a weapon.

It is also, most importantly, a beginning. As the Information Age hurtles along, as constant exposure to unverified claims and stories only accelerates, critical thought becomes increasingly vital, and increasingly rare. We must always ask ourselves *why* someone is telling us one thing or another, *why* one narrative or another becomes the official story printed in textbooks or carved into placards in museums. We must ask the questions those in power would rather not answer.

And we must do this together. We're grateful for everyone who accompanied us on the unpredictable journey, and we cannot wait for the adventures ahead. This book focuses primarily on proven conspiracies on the part of large businesses and the US government, which means it is only one part of a much larger story. There's much more to be done, and we'd love for you—specifically you—to be a part of it. You can find our show wherever you find your favorite podcasts, and if you listen, you'll find a way to contact us directly.

Ben Bowlin, December 8, 2021
Twitter: @BenBowlinHSW
Instagram: @benbowlin

ACKNOWLEDGMENTS

THIS BOOK IS THE RESULT OF A UNIQUE COLLABORATION, one that could not exist without the tireless efforts and deep insights of people like Nils Parker, Byrd Leavell, Zachary Wagman, Nick Benson, and every person that tuned in to the *Stuff They Don't Want You to Know* podcast or video series over the course of the past decade. In a way, you could say this book has millions of authors, people from across the planet with one common, unifying belief: the truth is out there. There is always more to the story, and if we dig deep enough, we can find that truth together.

Matt Frederick dedicates this book to his son, Ryder. Noel Brown dedicates this book to his daughter, Eden. Ben Bowlin dedicates this book to his mother, Susan Bowlin, who passed shortly before it came to print.

Love you, Mom.